# THE EPISTLES OF ST. IGNATIUS OF ANTIOCH



Complete Writings with Historical and Theological Commentary

**Published by**
**GRAPEVINE BOOKS**

www.grapevinebooks.com
email: contact@grapevinebooks.com

**Ordering Information:**
Quantity sales: Special discounts are available on quantity purchases by corporations, associations, and others.
For details, reach out to the publisher.

First published by Grapevine Books, 2025

## Contents

# The Epistle of Ignatius to the Ephesians

## Prologue

Ignatius, who is also Theophorus, unto her which hath been blessed in greatness through the plentitude of God the Father; which hath been foreordained before the ages to be forever and unto abiding and unchangeable glory, united and elect in a true passion, by the will of the Father and of Jesus Christ our God; even unto the church which is at Ephesus [of Asia], worthy of all felicitation; abundant greeting in Christ Jesus and in blameless joy.

## Chapter. 1

While I welcomed in God [your] well beloved name which ye bear by natural right, [in an upright and virtuous mind], by faith and love in Christ Jesus our Savior--being imitators of God, and having your hearts kindled in the blood of God, ye have perfectly fulfilled your congenial work--for when ye heard that I was on my way from Syria, in bonds for the sake of the common Name and hope, and was hoping through your prayers to succeed in fighting the wild beasts in Rome, that by so succeeding I might have power to be a disciple, ye were eager to visit me--seeing then in God's name I have received your whole multitude in the person of Onesimus, whose love passeth utterance and who is moreover your bishop [in the flesh] and I pray that ye may love him according to Jesus Christ and that ye all may be like him; for blessed is He that granted unto you according to your deserving to have such a bishop.

## Chapter. 2

But as touching my fellow servant Burrhus, who by the will of God is your deacon blessed in all things, I pray that he may remain with me to the honor of yourselves and of your bishop. Yea, and Crocus also, who is worthy of God and of you whom I received as an ensample of the love which ye bear me, hath relieved me in all ways--even so may the Father of Jesus Christ refresh him--together with Onesimus and Burrhus and Euplus and Fronto; in whom I saw you all with the eyes of love.

May I have joy of you always, if so be I an worthy of it. It is therefore meet for you in every way to glorify Jesus Christ who glorified you; that being perfectly joined together in one submission, submitting yourselves to your bishop and presbytery, ye may be sanctified in all things.

## Chapter. 3

I do not command you, as though I were somewhat. For even though I am in bonds for the Name's sake, I am not yet perfected in Jesus Christ. [For] now am I beginning to be a disciple; and I speak to you as to my school-fellows. For I ought to be trained by you for the contest in faith, in admonition, in endurance, in long-suffering.

But, since love doth not suffer me to be silent concerning you, therefore was I forward to exhort you, that ye run in harmony with the mind of God: for Jesus Christ also, our inseparable life, is the mind of the Father, even as the bishops that are settled in the farthest parts of the earth are in the mind of Jesus Christ.

## Chapter. 4

So then it becometh you to run in harmony with the mind of the bishop; which thing also ye do. For your honorable presbytery, which is worthy of God, is attuned to the bishop, even as its strings to a lyre. Therefore in your concord and harmonious love Jesus Christ is sung.

And do ye, each and all, form yourselves into a chorus, that being harmonious in concord and taking the key note of God ye may in unison sing with one voice through Jesus Christ unto the Father, that He may both hear you and acknowledge you by your good deeds to be members of His Son. It is therefore profitable for you to be in blameless unity, that ye may also be partakers of God always.

## Chapter. 5

For if I in a short time had such converse with your bishop, which was not after the manner of men but in the Spirit, how much more do I congratulate you who are closely joined with him as the Church is with Jesus Christ and as Jesus Christ is with the Father, that all things may be harmonious in unity.

Let no man be deceived. If any one be not within the precinct of the altar, he lacketh the bread [of God]. For, if the prayer of one and another hath so great force, how much more that of the bishop and of the whole Church.

Whosoever therefore cometh not to the congregation, he doth thereby show his pride and hath separated himself; for it is written, God resisteth the proud. Let us therefore be careful not to resist the bishop, that by our submission we may give ourselves to God.

## Chapter. 6

And in proportion as a man seeth that his bishop is silent, let him fear him the more. For every one whom the Master of the household sendeth to be steward over His own house, we ought so to receive as Him that sent him. Plainly therefore we ought to regard the bishop as the Lord Himself.

Now Onesimus of his own accord highly praiseth your orderly conduct in God, for that ye all live according to truth, and that no heresy hath a home among you: nay, ye do not so much as listen to any one, if he speak of aught else save concerning Jesus Christ in truth.

## Chapter. 7

For some are wont of malicious guile to hawk about the Name, while they do certain other things unworthy of God. These men ye ought to shun, as wild-beasts; for they are mad dogs, biting by stealth; against whom ye ought to be on your guard, for they are hard to heal.

There is one only physician, of flesh and of spirit, generate and in- generate, God in man, true Life in death, Son of Mary and Son of God, first passible and then impassible, Jesus Christ our Lord.

## Chapter. 8

Let no one therefore deceive you, as indeed ye are not deceived, seeing that ye belong wholly to God. For when no lust is established in you, which hath power to torment you, then truly ye live after God. I devote myself for you, and I dedicate myself as an offering for the church of you Ephesians which is famous unto all the ages.

They that are of the flesh cannot do the things of the Spirit, neither can they that are of the Spirit do the things of the flesh; even as faith cannot do the things of unfaithfulness, neither unfaithfulness the things of the faith. Nay, even those things which ye do after the flesh are spiritual; for ye do all things in Jesus Christ.

## Chapter. 9

But I have learned that certain persons passed through you from yonder, bringing evil doctrine; whom ye suffered not to sow seed in you, for ye stopped your ears, so that ye might not receive the seed sown by them; forasmuch as ye are stones of a temple, which were prepared beforehand for a building of God the Father, being hoisted up to the heights through the engine of Jesus Christ, which is the Cross, and using for a rope the Holy Spirit; while your faith is your windlass, and love is the way that leadeth up to God.

So then ye are all companions in the way, carrying your God and your shrine, your Christ and your holy things, being arrayed from head to foot in the commandments of Jesus Christ. And I too, taking part in the festivity, am permitted by letter to bear you company and to rejoice with you, that ye set not your love on anything after the common life of men, but only on God.

## Chapter. 10

And pray ye also without ceasing for the rest of mankind (for there is in them a hope of repentance), that they may find God. Therefore permit them to take lessons at least from your works.

Against their outbursts of wrath be ye meek; against their proud words be ye humble; against their railings set ye your prayers; against their errors be ye steadfast in the faith; against their fierceness be ye gentle. And be not zealous to imitate them by requital.

Let us show ourselves their brothers by our forbearance; but let us be zealous to be imitators of the Lord, vying with each other who shall suffer the greater wrong, who shall be defrauded, who shall be set at nought; that no herb of the devil be found in you: but in all purity and temperance abide ye in Christ Jesus, with your flesh and with your spirit.

## Chapter. 11

These are the last times. Henceforth let us have reverence; let us fear the long-suffering of God, lest it turn into a judgment against us. For either let us fear the wrath which is to come or let us love the grace which now is--the one or the other; provided only that we be found in Christ Jesus unto true life.

Let nothing glitter in your eyes apart from Him, in whom I carry about my bonds, my spiritual pearls in which I would fain rise again through your prayer, whereof may it be my lot to be always a partaker, that I may be found in the company of those Christians of Ephesus who moreover were ever of one mind with the Apostles in the power of Jesus Christ.

## Chapter. 12

I know who I am and to whom I write. I am a convict, ye have received mercy: I am in peril, ye are established.

Ye are the high-road of those that are on their way to die unto God. Ye are associates in the mysteries with Paul, who was sanctified, who obtained a good report, who is worthy of all felicitation; in whose foot-steps I would fain be found treading, when I shall attain unto God; who in every letter maketh mention of you in Christ Jesus.

## Chapter. 13

Do your diligence therefore to meet together more frequently for thanksgiving to God and for His glory. For when ye meet together frequently, the powers of Satan are cast down; and his mischief cometh to nought in the concord of your faith.

There is nothing better than peace, in which all warfare of things in heaven and things on earth is abolished.

## Chapter. 14

None of these things is hidden from you, if ye be perfect in your faith and love toward Jesus Christ, for these are the beginning and end of life--faith is the beginning and love is the end--and the two being found in unity are God, while all things else follow in their train unto true nobility.

No man professing faith sinneth, and no man possessing love hateth. The tree is manifest from its fruit; so they that profess to be Christ's shall be seen through their actions. For the Work is not a thing of profession now, but is seen then when one is found in the power of faith unto the end.

## Chapter. 15

It is better to keep silence and to be, than to talk and not to be. It is a fine thing to teach, if the speaker practice. Now there is one teacher, who spake and it came to pass: yea and even the things which He hath done in silence are worthy of the Father.

He that truly possesseth the word of Jesus is able also to hearken unto His silence, that he may be perfect; that through his speech he may act and through his silence he may be known.

Nothing is hidden from the Lord, but even our secrets are nigh unto Him. Let us therefore do all things as knowing that He dwelleth in us, to the end that we may be His temples and He Himself may be in us as our God. This is so, and it will also be made clear in our sight from the love which we rightly bear towards Him.

## Chapter. 16

Be not deceived, my brethren. Corrupters of houses shall not inherit the kingdom of God.

If then they which do these things after the flesh are put to death, how much more if a man through evil doctrine corrupt the faith of God for which Jesus Christ was crucified. Such a man, having defiled himself, shall go into the unquenchable fire; and in like manner also shall he that hearkeneth unto him.

## Chapter. 17

For this cause the Lord received ointment on His head, that He might breathe incorruption upon the Church. Be not anointed with the ill odor of the teaching of the prince of this world, lest he lead you captive and rob you o the life which is set before you.

And wherefore do we not all walk prudently, receiving the knowledge of God, which is Jesus Christ? Why perish we in our folly, not knowing the gift of grace which the Lord hath truly sent?

## Chapter. 18

My spirit is made an offscouring for the Cross, which is a stumbling-block to them that are unbelievers, but to us salvation and life eternal. Where is the wise? Where is the disputer? Where is the boasting of them that are called prudent?

For our God, Jesus the Christ, was conceived in the womb by Mary according to a dispensation, of the seed of David but also of the Holy Ghost; and He was born and was baptized that by His passion He might cleanse water.

## Chapter. 19

And hidden from the prince of this world were the virginity of Mary and her child-bearing and likewise also the death of the Lord--three mysteries to be cried aloud--the which were wrought in the silence of God. How then were they made manifest to the ages?

A star shone forth in the heaven above all the stars; and its light was unutterable, and its strangeness caused amazement; and all the rest of the constellations with the sun and moon formed themselves into a chorus about the star; but the star itself far outshone them all; and there was perplexity to know whence came this strange appearance which was so unlike them.

From that time forward every sorcery and every spell was dissolved, the ignorance of wickedness vanished away, the ancient kingdom was pulled down, when God appeared in the likeness of man unto newness of everlasting life; and that which had been perfected in the counsels of God began to take effect. Thence all things were perturbed, because the abolishing of death was taken in hand.

## Chapter. 20

If Jesus Christ should count me worthy through your prayer, and it should be the Divine will, in my second tract, which I intend to write to you, I will further set before you the dispensation whereof I have begun to speak, relating to the new man Jesus Christ, which consisteth in faith towards Him and in love towards Him, in His passion and resurrection,

especially if the Lord should reveal aught to me. Assemble yourselves together in common, every one of you severally, man by man, in grace, in one faith and one Jesus Christ, who after the flesh was of David's race, who is Son of Man and Son of God, to the end that ye may obey the bishop and the presbytery without distraction of mind; breaking one bread, which is the medicine of immortality and the antidote that we should not die but live for ever in Jesus Christ.

## Chapter. 21

I am devoted to you and to those whom for the honor of God ye sent to Smyrna; whence also I write unto you with thanksgiving to the Lord, having love for Polycarp as I have for you also. Remember me, even as I would that Jesus Christ may also remember you.

Pray for the church which is in Syria, whence I am led a prisoner to Rome-- I who am the very last of the faithful there; according as I was counted worthy to be found unto the honor of God. Fare ye well in God the Father and in Jesus Christ our common hope.

# GREEK

## ΠΡΟΣ ΕΦΕΣΙΟΥΣ ΙΓΝΑΤΙΟΣ

Ἰγνάτιος ὁ καὶ Θεοφόρος, τῇ εὐλογημένῃ ἐν μεγέθει θεοῦ πατρὸς πληρώματι, τῇ προωρισμένῃ πρὸ αἰώνων εἶναι διὰ παντὸς εἰς δόξαν παράμονον ἄτρεπτον, ἡνωμένῃ καὶ ἐκλελεγμένῃ ἐν πάθει ἀληθινῷ, ἐν θελήματι τοῦ πατρὸς καὶ Ἰησοῦ Χριστοῦ τοῦ θεοῦ ἡμῶν, τῇ ἐκκλησίᾳ τῇ ἀξιομακρίστῳ, τῇ οὔσῃ ἐν Ἐφέσῳ τῆς Ἀσίας, πλεῖστα ἐν Ἰησοῦ Χριστῷ καὶ ἐν ἀμώμῳ χαρᾷ χαίρειν.

### I

1. Ἀποδεξάμενος ἐν θεῷ τὸ πολθαγάπητόν σου ὀνομα, ὃ κέτησθε φύσει δικαίᾳ κατὰ πίστιν καὶ ἀγάπην ἐν Χριστῷ Ἰησοῦ, τῷ σωτῆρι ἡμων· μιμηταὶ ὄντες θεοῦ, ἀναζωπυρήσαντες ἐν αἵματι θεοῦ τὸ συγγενικὸν ἔργον τελείως ἀπηρτίσατε· 2. ακούσαντες γὰρ δεδεμένον ἀπὸ Συρίας ὑπὲρ τοῦ κοινοῦ ὀνόματος καὶ ἐλπίδος, ἐλπίζοντα τῇ προσευχῇῃ ὑμων ἐπιτυχεῖν ἐν Ῥώμῃ θηριομαχῆσαι, ἵνα διὰ τοῦ ἐπιτυχεῖν δυνηθῶ μαθητὴς εἶναι, ἰδεῖν ἐσπουδάσατε· 3. ἐπεὶ οὖν τὴν πολυπλήθειαν ὑμων ἐν ὀνόματι θεοῦ ἀπείληφα ἐν Ὀνησίμῳ, τῷ ἐν ἀγάπῃ ἀδιηγήτῳ, ὑμῶν δὲ ἐπισκόπῳ, ὃν εὔχομαι κατὰ Ἰησοῦν Χριστὸν ὑμᾶς ἀγαπᾶν καὶ πάντας ὑμας αὐγῷ ἐν ὁμοιότητι εἶναι. εὐλογητὸς γὰρ ὁ χαρισάμενος ὑμῖν ἀξίοις οὖσι τοιοῦτον ἐπίσκοπον κεκτῆσθαι.

### II

1. Περὶ δὲ τοῦ συνδούλου μου Βούρρου, τοῦ κατὰ θεὸν διακόνου ὑμῶν ἐν πᾶσιν εὐλογημένου, εὔχομαι παραμεῖναι αὐτὸν εἰς τιμὴν ὑμῶν καὶ τοῦ ἐπισκόπου· καὶ Κρόκος δέ, ὁ θεοῦ ἄξιος καὶ ὑμῶν, ὃν ἐξεμπλάριον τῆς ἀφ' ὑμῶν ἀγάπης ἀπέλαβον, κατὰ πάντα με

ἀνέπαυσεν, ὡς καὶ αὐτὸν ὁ πατὴρ Ἰησοῦ Χριστοῦ ἀναψύξαι, ἅμα Ὀνησίμῳ καὶ Βούρρῳ καὶ Εὔπλῳ καὶ Φρόντωνι, δι' ὧν πάντας ὑμᾶς κατὰ ἀγάπην εἶδον. 2. ὀναίμην ὑμῶν διὰ παντός, ἐάνπερ ἄξιος ὦ. πρέπον οὖν ἐστὶν κατὰ πάντα τρόπον δοξάζειν Ἰησοῦν Χριστὸν τὸν δοξάσαντα ὑμᾶς, ἵνα ἐν μιᾷ ὑποταγῇ κατηρτισμένοι, ὑποτασσόμενοι τῷ ἐπισκόπῳ καὶ τῷ πρεσβυτερίῳ, κατὰ πάντα ἦτε ἡγιασμένοι.

## III

1. Οὐ διατάσσομαι ὑμῖν ὡς τις. εἰ γὰρ καὶ δέδεμαι ἐν τῷ ὀνόματι, οὔπω ἀπήρτισμαι ἐν Ἰησοῦ Χριστῷ· νῦν γὰρ ἀρχὴν ἔχω τοῦ μαθητεύεσθαι, καὶ προσλαλῶ ὑμῖν ὡς συνδιδασκαλίταις μου. ἐμὲ γὰρ ἔδει ὑφ' ὑμῶν ὑπαλειφθῆναι πίστει, νουθεσίᾳ, ὑπομονῇ, μακροθυμίᾳ. 2. ἀλλ' ἐπεὶ ἡ ἀγάπη οὐκ ἐᾷ με σιωπᾶν περὶ ὑμῶν, διὰ τοῦτο προέλαβον παρακαλεῖν ὑμᾶς, ὅπως συντρέχητε τῇ γνώμῃ τοῦ θεοῦ. καὶ γὰρ Ἰησοῦς Χριστός, τὸ ἀδιάκριτον ἡμῶν ζῆν, τοῦ πατρὸς ἡ γνώμη, ὡς καὶ οἱ ἐπίσκοποι, οἱ κατὰ τὰ πέρατα ὁρισθέντες, ἐν Ἰησοῦ Χριστοῦ γνώμῃ εἰσίν.

## IV

1. Ὅθεν πρέπει ὑμῖν συντρέχειν τῇ τοῦ ἐπι-σκόπου γνώμῃ ὅπερ καὶ ποιεῖτε. τὸ γὰρ ἀξιονόμαστον ὑμῶν πρεσβυτέριον, τοῦ θεοῦ ἄξιον, οὕτως συνήρμοσται τῷ ἐπισκόπῳ, ὡς χορδαὶ κιθάρᾳ. διὰ τοῦτο ἐν τῇ ὁμονοίᾳ ὑμῶν καὶ συμφώνῳ ἀγάπῃ Ἰησοῦς Χριστὸς ᾄδεται. 2. καὶ οἱ κατ' ἄνδρα δὲ χορὸς γίνεθε, ἵνα σύμωνοι ὄντες ἐν ὁμονοίᾳ, χρῶμα θεοῦ λαβόντες ἐν ἑνότητι, ᾄδητε ἐν φωνῇ μιᾷ διὰ Ἰησοῦ Χριστοῦ τῷ πατρί, ἵνα ὑμῶν καὶ ἀκούσῃ καὶ ἐπιγινώσκῃ, δι' ὧν εὖ πράσσετε, μέλη ὄντας τοῦ υἱοῦ αὐτοῦ. χρήσιμον οὖν ἐστὶν ὑμᾶς ἐν ἀμώμῳ ἑνότητι εἶναι, ἵνα καὶ θεοῦ

πάντοτε μετέχητε.

## V

1. Εἰ γὰρ ἐγὼ ἐν μικρῷ χρόνῳ τοιαύτην συνήθειαν ἔσχον πρὸς τὸν ἐπίσκοπον ὑμῶν, οὐκ ἀνθρωπίνην οὖσαν, ἀλλὰ πνευματικήν, πόσῳ μᾶλλον ὑμᾶς μακαρίζω τοὺς ἐγκεκραμένους οὕτως, ὡς ἡ ἐκκλησία Ἰησοῦ Χριστῷ, καὶ ὡς Ἰησοῦς Χριστὸς τῷ πατρί, ἵνα πάντα ἐν ἑνότητι σύμφωνα ᾖ; 2. μηδεὶς πλανάσθω· ἐὰν μὴ τις ᾖ ἐντος τοῦ θυσιαστηρίου, ὑστερεῖται τοῦ ἄρτου τοῦ θεοῦ. εἰ γὰρ ἑνὸς καὶ δευτέρου προσευχὴ τοσαύτην ἰσχὺν ἔχει, πόσῳ μᾶλλον ἥ τε τοῦ ἐπισκόπου καὶ πάσης τῆς ἐκκλησίας; 3. ὁ οὖν μὴ ἐρχομενος ἐπί τὸ αὐτὸ οὗτος ἤδη ὑπερηφανει καὶ ἑαυτὸν διέκρινεν. γέγραπται γάρ· Ὑπερηφάνοις ὁ θεὸς ἀντιτάσσεται, σπουδάσωμεν οὖν μὴ ἀντιτάσσεσθαι τῷ ἐπι-σκόπῳ, ἵνα ὦμεν θεῷ ὑποτασσόμενοι.

## VI

1. Καὶ ὅσον βλέπει τις σιγῶντα ἐπίσκοπον, πλειόνως αὐτὸν φοβείσθω· πάντα γάρ, ὃν πέμπει ὁ οἰκοδεσπότης εἰς ἰδίαν οἰκονομίαν, οὕτως δεῖ ἡμᾶς αὐτὸν δέχεχθαι, ὡς αὐτὸν τὸν πέμψαντα. τὸν οὖν ἐπίσκοπον δῆλον ὅτι ὡς αὐτὸν κύριον δεῖ προσβλέπειν. 2. αὐτὸς μὲν οὖν Ὀνήσιμος ὑπερ-επαινεῖ ὑμῶν τὴν ἐν θεῷ εὐταξίαν, ὅτι πάντες κατὰ ἀλήθειαν ζῆτε καὶ ὅτι ἐν ὑμῖν οὐδεμία αἵρεσις καοικεῖ· ἀλλ᾽ οὐδὲ ἀκούετέ τινος πλέον, ἢ περὶ Ἰησοῦ Χριστοῦ λαλοῦντος ἐν ἀληθείᾳ.

## VII

1. Εἰώθασιν γάρ τινες δόλῳ πονηρῷ τὸ ὄνομα περιφέρειν, ἄλλα τινὰ πράσσοντες ἀνάξια θεοῦ· οὓς δεῖ ὑμᾶς ὡς θηρία ἐκκλίνειν· εἰσὶν γὰρ κύνες λυσσῶντες, λαθροδῆκται· οὓς δεῖ ὑμᾶς φθλάσσεσθαι ὄντας δυσθεραπεύτος. 2. εἷς ἰατρός ἐστιν, σαρκικός τε καὶ πνευματικός, γεννητὸς καὶ ἀγέννητος, ἐν ἀνθρώπῳ θεός, ἐν θανάτῳ ζωὴ ἀληθινή, καὶ ἐκ Μαριας καὶ ἐκ θεοῦ, πρῶτον παθητὸς καὶ τότε ἀπαθής, Ἰησοῦς Χριστὸς ὁ κύριος ἡμῶν.

## VIII

1. Μὴ οὖν τις ὑμᾶς ἐξαπατάτω, ὥσπερ οὐδὲ ἐξαπατᾶσθε, ὅλοι ὄντες θεοῦ. ὅταν γὰρ μηδεμία ἔρις ἐνήρεισται ἐν ὑμῖν ἡ δυναμένη ὑμᾶς βασανίσαι, ἄρα κατὰ θεὸν ζῆτε. περίψημα ὑμῶν καὶ ἁγνίζομαι ὑμῶν Ἐφεσίων, ἐκκλησίας τῆς διαβοή-του τοῖς αἰῶσιν. 2. οἱ σαρκικοὶ τὰ πνευματικὰ πράσσειν οὐ δύναται, οὐδὲ οἱ πνευματικοὶ τὰ σαρκικά, ὥσπερ οὐδὲ ἡ πίστις τὰ τῆς ἀπιστίας οὐδε ἡ ἀπιστία τὰ τῆς πίστεως. ἃ δὲ καὶ κατὰ σάρκα πράσσετε, ταῦτα πνευματικά ἐστιν· ἐν Ἰησοῦ γὰρ Χριστῷ πάντα πράσσετε.

## IX

1. Ἔγνων δὲ παροδεύσαντάς τινας ἐκεῖθεν, ἔχον-τας κακὴν διδαχήν· οὓς οὐκ εἰάσατε σπεῖραι εἰς ὑμᾶς, βύσαντες τὰ ὦτα, εἰς τὸ μὴ παραδέξασθαι τὰ σπειρόμενα ὑπ' αὐτῶν, ὡς ὄντες λίθοι ναοῦ πατρός, ἡτοιμασμένοι εἰς οἰκοδομὴν θεοῦ πατρός, αναφερόμενοι εἰς τὰ ὕψη διὰ τῆς μηχανῆς Ἰησοῦ Χριστοῦ, ὅς ἐστιν σταυρός, σψοινίῳ ψρώμενοι τῷ πνεύματι τῷ ἁγίῳ· ἡ δὲ πίστις ὑμῶν ἀναγωγεὺς ὑμῶν, ἡ δὲ ἀγάπη ὁδὸς ἡ ἀναφέρουσα εἰς θεόν. 2. ἐστὲ οὖν καὶ σύνοδοι πάντες, θεοφόροι καὶ ναοφόροι, χριστοφόροι, ἁγιοφόροι, κατὰ πάντα κεκοσμημένοι ἐντολαῖς Ἰησοῦ Χριστοῦ· οἷς καὶ ἀγαλλιώμενος ἠξιώθην δι' ὧν γράφω

προσομιλῆσαι ὑμῖν καὶ συγχαρῆναι, ὅτι κατ' ἀνθρωπων βίον οὐδὲν ἀγαπᾶτε εἰ μὴ μόνον τὸν θεόν.

## X

1. Καὶ ὑπὲρ τῶν ἄλλων δὲ ἀνθρώπων ἀδια-λείπτως προσεύχεσθε, ἔστιν γὰρ ἐν αὐτοῖς ἐλπὶς μετανοίας, ἵνα θεοῦ τύχωσιν. ἐπιτρέψατε οὖν αὐτοῖς κἂν ἐκ τῶν ἔργων ὑμῖν μαθητευθῆναι. 2. πρὸς τὰς ὀργὰς αὐτῶν ὑμεῖς πραεῖς, πρὸς τὰς μεγαλορημοσύνας αὐτῶν ὑμεῖς ταπεινόφρονες, πρὸς τὰς βλασφημίας αὐτῶν ὑμεῖς τὰς προσευχάς, πρὸς τὴν πλαπνην αὐτῶν ὑμεῖς ἥμεροι, μὴ σπουδάζοντες ἀντιμιμήσασθαι αὐτούς. 3. ἀδελφοὶ αὐτῶν εὑρεθῶμεν τῇ ἐπιειδειᾳ· μιμηταὶ δὲ τοῦ κυρίου σπου-δάζωμεν εἶναι, τίς πλέον ἀδικηθῇ, τίς ἀποστερηθῇ, τίς ἀθετηθῇ· ἵνα μὴ τοῦ διαβόλου βοτάνη τις εὑρεθῇ ἐν ὑμῖν, ἀλλ' ἐν πάσῃ ἁγνείᾳ καὶ σωφροσύνῃ μένητε ἐν Ἰησοῦ Χριστῷ σαρκικῶς καὶ πνευματικῶς.

## XI

1. Ἔσχατοι καιροί, λοιπὸν αἰσχυνθῶμεν, φοβηθῶμεν τὴν μακροθυμίαν τοῦ θεοῦ, ἵνα μὴ ἡμῖν εἰς κρίμα γένηται. ἢ γὰρ τὴν μέλλουσαν ὀργὴν φοβη-θῶμεν, ἢ τὴν ἐνεστῶσαν χάριν ἀγαπηπσωμεν, ἓν τῶν δύο· μόνον ἐν Χριτῷ Ἰησοῦ εὑρεθῆναι εἰς τὸ ἀληθινὸν ζῆν. 2. χωρὶς τούτου μηδὲν ὑμῖν πρεπέτω, ἐν ᾧ τὰ δεσμὰ περιφέρω, τοὺς πνευματικοὺς μαργαρίτας, ἐν οἷς γένοιτό μοι ἀνατῆναι τῇ προσευχῇ ὑμῶν, ἧς γένοιτό μοι ἀεὶ μέταχον εἶναι, ἵνα ἐν κλήρῳ Ἐφεσίων εὑρεθῶ τῶν Χριστιανῶν, οἱ καὶ τοῖς ἀποστόλοις πάντοτε συνῄνεσαν ἐν δυνάμει Ἰησοῦ Χριστοῦ.

## XII

1. Οἶδα, τίς εἰμι καὶ τίσιν γράφω. ἐγὼ κατάκριτος, ὑμεῖς ἠλεημένοι· ἐγὼ ὑπὸ κίνδυνον, ὑμεῖς ἐστηρυγμένοι· 2. πάροδός ἐστε τῶν εἰς θεὸν ἀναιρουμένων, Παύλου συμμύσται τοῦ ἡγιασμένου, τοῦ μεμαρτυρημένον, ἀξιομακαρίστον, οὗ γένοιτό μοι ὑπὸ τὰ ἴχνη εὑρεθῆναι, ὅταν θεοῦ ἐπιτύχω, ὃς ἐν πάσῃ ἐπιστολῇ μνημονεύει ὑμῶν ἐν Χριστῷ Ἰησοῦ.

## XIII

1. Σπουδάζετε οὖν πυκνότερον συνέρχεσθαι εἰς εὐχαριστίαν θεοῦ καὶ εἰς δόξαν. ὅταν γὰρ πυκνῶς ἐπὶ τὸ αὐτὸ γίνεσθε, καθαιροῦνται αἱ δυνάμεις τοῦ Χατανᾶ, καὶ λύεται ὁ ὄλεθρος αὐτοῦ ἐν τῇ ὁμονοίᾳ ὑμῶν τῆς πίστεως. 2. οὐδέν ἐστιν ἄμεινον εἰρήνης, ἐν ᾗ πᾶς πόλεμος καταργεῖται ἐπουραίων καὶ ἐπιγείων.

## XIV

1. Ὧν οὐδεν λανθάνει ὑμᾶς, ἐὰν τελείως εἰς Ἰησοῦ Χριστὸν ἔχητε τὴν πίστιν καὶ τήν ἀγάπην, ἥτις ἐστὶν ἀρχὴ ζωῆς καὶ τέλος· ἀρχὴ μὲν πίστις, τέλος δὲ ἀγάπη. τὰ δὲ δύο ἐν ἑνοτητι γενόμενα θεός ἐστιν, τὰ δὲ ἀλλα πάντα εἰς καλοκἀγαθίαν ακόλουθά ἐστιν. 2. οὐδεὶς πίστιν ἐπαγγελλόμενος ἁμαρτάνει, οὐδὲ ἀγάπην κεκτημένος μισεῖ. φανερὸν τὸ δένδρον ἀπὸ τοῦ καρποῦ αὐτοῦ. οὕτως οἱ ἐπαγ-γελλόμενοι Χριστοῦ εἶναι δι᾽ ὧν πράσσουσιν ὀφθήσονται. οὐ γὰρ νῦν ἐπαγγελίας τὸ ἔργον, ἀλλ᾽ ἐν δυνάμει πίστεως ἐάν τις εὑρεθῇ εἰς τέλος.

## XV

1. Ἄμεινόν ἐστιν σιωπᾶν καὶ εἶναι, ἢ λαλοῦντα μὴ εἶναι. καλὸν

τὸ διδάσκειν, ἐὰν ὁ λέγων ποιῇ. εἷς οὖν διδάσκαλος, ὃς εἶπεν, καὶ ἐγένετο· καὶ ἃ σιγῶν δὲ πεποίηκεν ἄξια τοῦ πατρός ἐστιν. 2. ὁ λόγον Ἰησοῦ κεκτημένος ἀληθῶς δύναται καὶ τῆς ἡσυχιας αὐτοῦ ἀκούειν, ἵνα τέλειος ᾖ, ἵνα δι' ὧν λαλεῖ πράσσῃ καὶ δι' ὧν σιγᾷ γινώσκηται. 3. οὐδὲν λανθάνει τὸν κύριον, ἀλλὰ καὶ τὰ κρυπτὰ ἡμῶν ἐγγυς αὐτῷ ἐστιν, πάντα οὖν ποιῶμεν ὡς αὐτοῦ ἐν ἡμῖν κατοικοῦντος, ἵνα ὦμεν αὐτοῦ ναοὶ καὶ αὐτὸς ἐν ἡμῖν θεὸς ἡμῶν· ὅπερ καὶ ἔστιν καὶ φανήσεται πρὸ προσώπου ἡμῶν, ἐξ ὧν δικαίως ἀαπῶμεν αὐτον.

## XVI

1. Μὴ πλανᾶσθε, ἀδελφοί μου· οἱ οἰκοφθόροι βασιλείαν θεοῦ οὐ κληρονομήσουσιν. 2. εἰ οὖν οἱ κατὰ σάρκα ταῦτα πράσσοντες ἀπέθανον, πόσῳ μᾶλλον, ἐὰν πίστιν θεοῦ ἐν κακῇ διδασκαλίᾳ φθείρῃ, ὑπὲρ ἧς Ἰησοῦς Χριστὸς ἐσταυρώθη; ὁ τοιοῦτος ῥυπαρὸς γενόμενος, εἰς τὸ πῦρ τὸ ἄσβεστον χωρήσει, ὁμοίως καὶ ὁ ἀκούων αὐτου.

## XVII

1. Διὰ τοῦτο μύρον ἔλαβεν ἐπὶ τῆς κεφαλῆς αὐτοῦ ὁ κύριος, ἵνα πνέῃ τῇ ἐκκλησίᾳ ἀφθαρσίαν. μὴ ἀλείφεσθε δυσωδίαν τῆς διδασκαλίας τοῦ ἄρχοντος τοῦ αἰῶνος τούτου, μὴ αἰχμαλωτίσῃ ὑμᾶς ἐκ τοῦ προκειμένου ζῆν. 2. διὰ τί δὲ οὐ πάντες φρόνιμοι γινόμεθα λαβόντες θεοῦ γνῶσιν, ὁ ἐστιν Ἰησοῦς Χριστός; τί μωρῶς ἀπολλύμεθα, αγνοοῦντες τὸ χάρισμα, ὃ πεππομφεν ἀληθῶς ὁ κύριος;

## XVIII

1. Περίψημα τὸ ἐμὸν πνεῦμα τοῦ σταυροῦ, ὃ ἐστιν σκάνδαλον τοῖς ἀπιστοῦσιν, ἡμῖν δὲ σωτηρία καὶ ζωὴ αἰώνιος. ποῦ σωφός; ποῦ συζητητής; ποῦ καύχησις τῶν λεγομένων συνετῶν; 2. ὁ γὰρ θεὸς ἡμῶν Ἰησοῦς ὁ Χριστὸς ἐκυοφορήθη ὑπὸ Μαρίας κατ' οἰκονομίαν θεοῦ ἐκ σπέρματος μὲν Δαυείδ, πνεύματος δὲ ἁγίου· ὃς ἐγεννήθη καὶ ἐβαπτίσθη, ἵνα τῷ πάθει τὸ ὕδωρ καθαρίσῃ.

## XIX

1. Καὶ ἔλαθεν τὸν ἄρχοντα τοῦ αἰῶνος τούτου ἡ παρθενία Μαρίας καὶ ὁ τοκετὸς αὐτῆς, ὁμοίως καὶ ὁ θάνατος τοῦ κυρίου· τρία μυστήρια κραυγῆς, ἅτινα ἐν ἡσυχίᾳ θεοῦ ἐπράχθη. 2. πῶς οὖν ἐφανερώθη τοῖς αἰῶσιν; ἀστὴρ ἐν οὐρανῷ ἔλαμψεν ὑπὲρ πάντας τοὺς ἀστέρας, καὶ τὸ φῶς αὐτοῦ ἀνεκλάλητον ἦν καὶ ξενισμὸν παρεῖχεν ἡ καινότης αὐτοῦ, τὰ δὲ λοιπὰ πάντα ἄστρα ἅμα ἡλίῳ καὶ σελήνῃ χορὸς ἐγένετο τῷ ἀστέρι, αὐτὸς δὲ ἦν ὑπερβάλλων τὸ φῶς αὐτοῦ ὑπὲρ΄πάντα· ταραχή τε ἦν, πόθεν ἡ καινότης ἡ ἀνόμοιος αὐτοῖς. 3. ὅθεν ἐλύετο πᾶσα μαγεία καὶ΄πᾶς δεσμὸς ἠφανίζετο κακίας· ἄγνοια καθῃρεῖτο, παλαιὰ βασι-λεία διεφθείρετο θεοῦ ἀνθρωπίνως φανερουμένου εἰς καινότητα ἀϊδίου ζωῆς· ἀρχὴν δὲ ἐλάμβανεν τὸ παρὰ θεῷ ἀπηρτισμένον. ἔνθεν τὰ πάντα συνεκινεῖτο διὰ τὸ μελετᾶσθαι θανάτου κατάλυσιν.

## XX

1. Ἐάν με καταξιώσῃ Ἰησοῦς Χριστὸς ἐν τῇ προσευχῇ ὑμῶν καὶ θέλημα ᾖ, ἐν τῷ δευτέρῳ βιβλιδίῳ, ὃ μέλλω γράφειν ὑμῖν, προσδηλώσω ὑμῖν, ἧς ἠρξάμην οἰκονομίας εἰς τὸν καινὸν ἄνθρωπον Ἰησοῦν Χριστόν, ἐν τῇ αὐτου πίστει καὶ ἐν τῇ αὐτοῦ ἀγαπῃ, ἐν πάθει αὐτοῦ καὶ ἀναστάσει· 2. μάλιστα ἐὰν ὁ κύριος μοι ἀποκαλύψῃ, ὅτι οἱ κατ' ἄνδρα κοινῇ πάντες ἐν χάριτι ἐξ ὀνόματος συνέρχεσθε ἐν μιᾷ πίστει καὶ ἐν Ἰησοῦ Χριστῷ, τῷ κατὰ σάρκα ἐκ γένους Δαυείδ, τῷ ἀνθρώπου καὶ υἱῷ θεοῦ, εἰς τὸ ὑπακούειν ὑμᾶς τῷ ἐπισκόπῳ καὶ τῷ πρεσβυτερίῳ ἀπερισπάστῳ κιανοίᾳ, ἕνα ἄρτον κλῶντες, ὅς ἐστιν φάρμακον ἀθανασιας, ἀντίδοτος τοῦ μὴ ἀποθανεῖν, ἀλλὰ ζῆν ἐν Ἰησοῦ Χριστῷ διὰ παντός.

## XXI

1. Ἀντίψυχον ὑμῶν ἐγὼ καὶ ὧν ἐπέμψατε εἰς θεοῦ τιμὴν εἰς Σμύρναν, ὅθεν καὶ γράφω ὑμῖν, εὐχαριστῶν τῷ κυρίῳ, ἀγαπῶν Πολύκαρπον ὡς καὶ ὑμᾶς· μνημονεύετέ μου, ὡς καὶ ὑμῶν Ἰησοῦς Χριστός. 2. προσεύχεσθε ὑπὲρ τῆς ἐκκλησίας τῆς ἐν Συρίᾳ, ὅθεν δεδεμένος εἰς Ῥώμην ἀπάγομαι, ἔσχατος ὢν τῶν ἐκεῖ πιστῶν, ὥσπερ ἠξιώθην εἰς τιμὴν θεοῦ εὑρεθῆναι. ἔρρωσθε ἐν θεῷ πατρὶ καὶ ἐν Ἰησοῦ Χριστῷ, τῇ κοινῇ ἐλπίδι ἡμῶν.

# The Epistle of Ignatius to the Magnesians

## Chapter. Prologue

Ignatius, who is also Theophorus, unto her which hath been blessed through the grace of God the Father in Christ Jesus our Savior, in whom I salute the church which is in Magnesia on the Maeander, and I wish her abundant greeting in God the Father and in Jesus Christ.

## Chapter. 1

When I learned the exceeding good order of your love in the ways of God, I was gladdened and I determined to address you in the faith of Jesus Christ.

For being counted worthy to bear a most godly name, in these bonds, which I carry about, I sing the praise of the churches; and I pray that there may be in them union of the flesh and of the spirit which are Jesus Christ's, our never-failing life--and union of faith and of love which is preferred before all things, and--what is more than all--an union with Jesus and with the Father, in whom if we endure patiently all the despite of the prince of this world and escape therefrom, we shall attain unto God.

## Chapter. 2

Forasmuch then as I was permitted to see you in the person of Damas your godly bishop and your worthy presbyters Bassus and Apollonius and my fellow-servant the deacon Zotion, of whom I would fain have joy, for that he is subject to the bishop as unto the grace of God and to the presbytery as unto the law of

Jesus Christ:--

## Chapter. 3

Yea, and it becometh you also not to presume upon the youth of your bishop, but according to the power of God the Father to render unto him all reverence, even as I have learned that the holy presbyters also have not taken advantage of his outwardly youthful estate, but give place to him as to one prudent in God; yet not to him, but to the Father of Jesus Christ, even to the Bishop of all.

For the honor therefore of Him that desired you, it is meet that ye should be obedient without dissimulation. For a man doth not so much deceive this bishop who is seen, as cheat that other who is invisible; and in such a case he must reckon not with flesh but with God who knoweth the hidden things.

## Chapter. 4

It is therefore meet that we not only be called Christians, but also be such; even as some persons have the bishop's name on their lips, but in everything act apart from him. Such men appear to me not to keep a good conscience, for as much as they do not assemble themselves together lawfully according to commandment.

## Chapter. 5

Seeing then that all things have an end, and these two life and death--are set before us together, and each man shall go to his own place; for just as there are two coinages, the one of God and the other of the world, and each of them hath its proper stamp impressed upon it, the unbelievers the stamp of this world, but the faithful in love the stamp of God the Father through Jesus Christ, through whom unless of our own free choice we accept to die unto His passion, His life is not in us:--

## Chapter. 6

Seeing then that in the aforementioned persons I beheld your whole people in faith and embraced them, I advise you, be ye zealous to do all things in godly concord, the bishop presiding after the likeness of God and the presbyters after the likeness of the council of the Apostles, with the deacons also who are most dear to me, having been entrusted with the diaconate of Jesus Christ, who was with the Father before the worlds and appeared at the end of time.

Therefore do ye all study conformity to God and pay reverence one to another; and let no man regard his neighbor after the flesh, but love ye one another in Jesus Christ always. Let there be nothing among you which shall have power to divide you, but be ye united with the bishop and with them that preside over you as an ensample and a lesson of incorruptibility.

## Chapter. 7

Therefore as the Lord did nothing without the Father, [being united with Him], either by Himself or by the Apostles, so neither do ye anything without the bishop and the presbyters. And attempt not to think anything right for yourselves apart from others: but let there be one prayer in common, one supplication, one mind, one hope, in love and in joy unblamable, which is

Jesus Christ, than whom there is nothing better.

Hasten to come together all of you, as to one temple, even God; as to one altar, even to one Jesus Christ, who came forth from One Father and is with One and departed unto One.

## Chapter. 8

Be not seduced by strange doctrines nor by antiquated fables, which are profitless. For if even unto this day we live after the manner of Judaism, we avow that we have not received grace:

for the divine prophets lived after Christ Jesus. For this cause also they were persecuted, being inspired by His grace to the end that they which are disobedient might be fully persuaded that there is one God who manifested Himself through Jesus Christ His Son, who is His Word that proceeded from silence, who in all things was well-pleasing unto Him that sent Him.

## Chapter. 9

If then those who had walked in ancient practices attained unto newness of hope, no longer observing Sabbaths but fashioning their lives after the Lord's day, on which our life also arose through Him and through His death which some men deny--a mystery whereby we attained unto belief, and for this cause we endure patiently, that we may be found disciples of Jesus Christ our only teacher--

if this be so, how shall we be able to live apart from Him? seeing that even the prophets, being His disciples, were expecting Him as their teacher through the Spirit. And for this cause He whom they rightly awaited, when He one, raised them from the dead.

## Chapter. 10

Therefore let us not be insensible to His goodness. For if He should imitate us according to our deeds, we are lost. For this cause, seeing that we are become His disciples, let us learn to live as beseemeth Christianity. For whoso is called by another name besides this, is not of God.

Therefore put away the vile leaven which hath waxed stale and sour, and betake yourselves to the new leaven, which is Jesus Christ. Be ye salted in Him, that none among you grow putrid, seeing that by your savor ye shall be proved.

It is monstrous to talk of Jesus Christ and to practice Judaism. For Christianity did not believe in Judaism, but Judaism in Christianity, wherein every tongue believed and was gathered together unto God.

## Chapter. 11

Now these things I say, my dearly beloved, not because I have learned that any of you are so minded; but as being less than any of you, I would have you be on your guard betimes, that ye fall not into the snares of vain doctrine; but be ye fully persuaded concerning the birth and the passion and the resurrection, which took place in the time of the governorship of Pontius Pilate; for these things were truly and certainly done by Jesus Christ our hope; from which hope may it not befall any of you to be turned aside.

## Chapter. 12

Let me have joy of you in all things, if I be worthy. For even though I am in bonds, yet am I not comparable to one of you who are at liberty. I know that ye are not puffed up; for ye have Jesus Christ in yourselves. And, when I praise you, I know that ye only feel the more shame; as it is written the righteous man is a self-accuser.

## Chapter. 13

Do your diligence therefore that ye be confirmed in the ordinances of the Lord and of the Apostles, that ye may prosper in all things whatsoever ye do in flesh and spirit, by faith and by love, in the Son and Father and in the Spirit, in the beginning and in the end, with your revered bishop, and with the fitly wreathed spiritual circlet of your presbytery, and with the deacons who walk after God.

Be obedient to the bishop and to one another, as Jesus Christ was to the Father [according to the flesh], and as the Apostles were to Christ and to the Father, that there may be union both of flesh and of spirit.

## Chapter. 14

Knowing that ye are full of God, I have exhorted you briefly.

Remember me in your prayers, that I may attain unto God; and remember also the church which is in Syria, whereof I am not worthy to be called a member. For I have need of your united prayer and love in God, that it may be granted to the church which is in Syria to be refreshed by the dew of your fervent supplication.

## Chapter. 15

The Ephesians from Smyrna salute you, from whence also I write to you. They are here with me for the glory of God, as also are ye; and they have comforted me in all things, together with Polycarp bishop of the Smyrnaeans. Yea, and all the other churches salute you in the honor of Jesus Christ. Fare ye well in godly concord, and possess ye a steadfast spirit, which is Jesus Christ.

# GREEK
# ΜΑΓΝΗΣΙΕΥΣΙΝ ΙΓΝΑΤΙΟΣ

Ἰγνάτιος, ὁ καὶ Θεοφόρος, τῇ εὐλογημένῃ ἐν χάριτι θεοῦ πατρὸς ἐν Χριστῷ Ἰησοῦ τῷ σωτῆρι ἡμῶν, ἐν ᾧ ἀσπάζομαι τὴν ἐκκλησίαν τὴν οὖσαν ἐν Μαγνησίᾳ τῇ πρὸς Μαιάνδρῳ καὶ εὔχομαι ἐν θεῷ πατρὶ καὶ ἐν Ἰησοῦ Χριστῷ πλεῖστα χαίρειν.

## I

1. Γνοὺς ὑμῶν τὸ πολυεύτακτον τῆς κατὰ θεὸν ἀγάπης, ἀγαλλιώμενος προειλόμην ἐν πίστει Ἰησοῦ Χριστοῦ προσλαλῆσαι ὑμῖν. 2. καταξιωθεὶς γὰρ ὀνόματος θεοπρεπεστάτου, ἐν οἷς περιφέρω δεσμοῖς ᾄ δω τὰς ἐκκλησίας, ἐν αἷς ἕνωσιν εὔχομαι σαρκὸς καὶ πνεύματος Ἰησοῦ Χριστοῦ, τοῦ διὰ παντὸς ἡμῶν ζῆν, πίστεώς τε καὶ ἀγάπης, ἧς οὐδὲν προκέκριται, τὸ δὲ κυριώτερον Ἰησοῦ και πατρός· ἐν ᾧ ὑπομένοντες τὴν πᾶσαν ἐπήρειαν τοῦ ἄρχοντος τοῦ αἰῶνος τούτου καὶ διαφυγόντες θεοῦ τευξόμεθα.

## II

1. Ἐπεὶ οὖν ἠξιώθην ἰδεῖν ὑμᾶς διὰ Δαμᾶ τοῦ ἀξιοθέον ὑμῶν ἐπισκόπου καὶ πρεσβυτέρων ἀξίων Βάσσου καὶ Ἀπολλωνίου καὶ τοῦ συνδούλου μου διακόνον Ζωτίωνος, οὗ ἐγὼ ὀναίμην, ὅτι ὑποτάσσεται τῷ ἐπισκόπῳ ὡς χάριτι θεοῦ καὶ τῷ πρεσβυτερίῳ ὡς νόμῳ Ἰησοῦ Χριστοῦ.

## III

1. Και ὑμῖν δὲ πρέπει μὴ συγχρᾶσθαι τῇ ἡλικίᾳ τοῦ ἐπισκόπου, ἀλλὰ κατὰ δύναμιν θεοῦ πατρὸς πᾶσαν ἐντροπὴν αὐτῷ ἀπονέμειν, καθὼς ἔγνων καὶ τοὺς ἁγίους πρεσβυτέρους οὐ προσειληφότας τὴν φαινομένην νεωτερικὴν τάξιν, ἀλλ' ὡς φρονίμους ἐν θεῷ συγχωροῦντας αὐτῷ, οὐκ αὐτῷ δέ, ἀλλὰ τῷ πατρὶ Ἰησοῦ Χριστοῦ, τῷ πάντων ἐπισκόπῳ. 2. εἰς τιμὴν οὖν ἐκείνου τοῦ θελήσαντος ἡμᾶς πρέπον ἐστὶν ἐπακούειν κατὰ μηδεμίαν ὑπόκρισιν· ἐπεὶ οὐχ ὅτι τὸν ἐπίσκοπον τοῦτον τὸν βλεπόμενον πλανᾷ τις, ἀλλὰ τὸν ἀόρατον παραλογίζεται. τὸ δὲ τοιοῦτον οὐ πρὸς σάρκα ὁ λόγος, ἀλλὰ πρὸς θεὸν τὸν τὰ κρύφια εἰδότα.

## IV

1. Πρέπον οὖν ἐστιν μὴ μόνον καλεῖσθαι Χριστιανούς, ἀλλὰ καὶ εἶναι· ὥσπερ καί τινες ἐπίσκοπον μὲν καλοῦσιν, χωρὶς δὲ αὐτοῦ πάντα πράσσουσιν. οἱ τοιοῦτοι δὲ οὐκ εὐσυνείδητοί μοι εἶναι φαίνονται διὰ τὸ μὴ βεβαίως κατ' ἐντολὴν συναθροίζεσθαι.

## V

1. Ἐπεὶ οὖν τέλος τὰ πράγματα ἔχει καὶ πρόκειται τὰ δύο ὁμοῦ, ὅ τε θάνατος καὶ ἡ ζωή, καὶ ἕκαστος εἰς τὸν ἴδιον τόπον μέλλει χωρεῖν· 2. ὥσπερ γάρ ἐστιν νομίσματα δύο, ὃ μὲν θεοῦ, ὃ δὲ κόσμου, καὶ ἕκαστον αὐτῶν ἴδιον χαρακτῆρα ἐπικείμενον ἔχει, οἱ ἄπιστοι τοῦ κόσμου τούτου, οἱ δὲ πιστοὶ ἐν ἀγάπῃ χαρακτῆρα θεοῦ πατρὸς διὰ Ἰησοῦ Χριστοῦ, δι' οὗ ἐὰν μὴ αὐθαιρέτως ἔχωμεν τὸ ἀποθανεῖν εἰς τὸ αὐτοῦ πάθος, τὸ ζῆν αὐτοῦ οὐκ ἔστιν ἐν ἡμῖν.

## VI

1. Ἐπεῖ οὖν ἐν τοῖς προγεγραμμένοις προσώποις τὸ πᾶν πλῆθος ἐθεώρησα ἐν πίστει καὶ ἠγάπησα, παραινῶ, ἐν ὁμονοίᾳ θεοῦ σπουδάζετε πάντα πράσσειν, προκαθημένου τοῦ ἐπισκόπου εἰς τόπον θεοῦ καὶ τῶν πρεσβυτέρων εἰς τόπον συνεδρίου τῶν ἀποστόλων, καὶ τῶν διακόνων τῶν ἐμοὶ γλυκυτάτων πεπιστευμένων διακονίαν Ἰησοῦ Χριστοῦ, ὃς πρὸ αἰώνων παρὰ πατρὶ ἦν καὶ ἐν τέλει ἐφάνη. 2. πάντες οὖν ὁμοήθειαν θεοῦ λαβόντες ἐντρέπεσθε ἀλληλους καὶ μηδεὶς κατὰ σάρκα βλεπέτω τὸν πλησίον, ἀλλ' ἐν Ἰησοῦ Χριστῷ ἀλληλους διὰ παντὸς ἀγαπᾶτε. μηδὲν ἔστω ἐν ὑμῖν, ὃ δυνήσεται ὑμᾶς μερίσαι ἀλλ' ἑνώθητε τῷ ἐπισκόπῳ καὶ τοῖς προκαθημένοις εἰς τύπον καὶ διδαχὴν ἀφθαρσίας.

## VII

1. Ὥσπερ οὖν ὁ κύριος ἄνευ τοῦ πατρὸς οὐδὲν ἐποίησεν, ἡνωμένος ὤν, οὔτε δι' ἑαυτοῦ οὔτε διὰ τῶν ἀποστόλων· οὕτως μηδὲ ὑμεῖς ἄνευ τοῦ ἐπισπόπου καὶ τῶν πρεσβυτέρων μηδὲν πράσσετε· μηδὲ πειράσητε εὔλογόν τι φαίνεσθαι ἰδίᾳ ὑμῖν, νοῦς, μία ἐλπὶς ἐν ἀγάπῃ, ἐν τῇ χαρᾷ τῇ ἀμώμῳ, ὅ ἐστιν Ἰησοῦς Χριστός, οὗ ἄμεινον οὐδέν ἐστιν. 2. πάντες ὡς εἰς ἕνα ναὸν συντρέχετε θεοῦ, ὡς ἐπὶ ἓν θυσιαστήριον, ἐπὶ ἕνα Ἰησοῦν Χριστόν, τὸν ἀφ' ἑνὸς πατρὸς προελθόντα καὶ εἰς ἕνα ὄντα καὶ χωρησαντα.

## VIII

1. Μὴ πλανᾶσθε ταῖς ἑτεροδοξίαις μηδὲ μυθεύμασιν τοῖς παλαιοῖς ἀνωφελέσιν οὖσιν. εἰ γὰρ μέχρι νῦν κατὰ Ἰουδαϊσμὸν ζῶμεν, ὁμολογοῦμεν χάριν μὴ εἰληφέναι. 2. οἱ γὰρ θειότατοι προφῆται

κατὰ Χριστὸν Ἰησοῦν ἔζησαν. διὰ τοῦτο καὶ ἐδιώχθησαν, ἐνπνεόμενοι ὑπὸ τῆς χάριτος αὐτοῦ, εἰς τὸ πληροφρηθῆναι τοὺς ἀπειθοῦντας, ὅτι εἷς τοῦ υἱοῦ αὐτοῦ, ὅς ἐστιν αὐτοῦ λόγος ἀπὸ σιγῆς προελθών, ὃς κατὰ πάντα εὐηρέστησεν τῷ πέμψαντι αὐτόν.

## IX

1. Εἰ οὖν οἱ ἐν παλαιοῖς πράγμασιν ἀναστρα. φέντες εἰς καινότητα ἐλπίδος ἦλθον, μηκέτι σαββατίζοντες, ἀλλὰ κατὰ κυριακὴν ζῶντες, ἐν ᾗ καὶ ἡ ζωὴ ἡμῶν ἀνέτειλεν δι' αὐτοῦ καὶ τοῦ θανάτου αὐτοῦ, ὅν τινες ἀρνοῦνται, δι' οὗ μυστηρίου ἐλάβομεν τὸ πιστεύειν, καὶ διὰ τοῦτο ὑπομένομεν, ἵνα εὑρεθῶμεν μαθηταὶ Ἰησοῦ Χριστοῦ τοῦ μόνου διδασκάλου ἡμῶν· 2. πῶς ἡμεῖς δυναησόμεθα δῆσαι χωρὶς αὐτοῦ, οὗ καὶ οἱ προφῆται μαθηταὶ ὄντες τῷ πνεύματι ὡς διδάσκαλον αὐτὸν προσεδόκων; καὶ διὰ τοῦτο, ὃν δικαίως ἀνέμενον, παρὼν ἤγειρεν αὐτοὺς ἐκ νεκρῶν.

## X

1. Μὴ οὖν ἀναισθητῶμεν τῆς ψρηστότητος αὐτοῦ. ἐὰν γὰρ ἡμᾶς μιμήσηται καθὰ πράσσομεν, οὐκέτι ἐσμέν. διὰ τοῦτο, μαθηταὶ αὐτοῦ γενόμενοι, μάθωμεν κατὰ Χριστιανισμὸν ζῆν. ὃς γὰρ ἄλλῳ ὀνόματι καλεῖται πλέον τούτου, οὐκ ἔστιν τοῦ θεοῦ. 2. ὑπέρθεσθε οὖν τὴν κακὴν ζύμην, τὴν παλαιωθεῖσαν καὶ ἐνοξίσασαν, καὶ Χριστός. ἁλίσθητε ἐν αὐτῷ, ἵνα μὴ διαφθαρῇ τις ἐν ὑμῖν, ἐπεὶ ἀπὸ τῆς τῆς ὀσμῆς ἐλεγχθήσεσθε. 3. ἄτοπόν ἐστιν, Ἰησοῦν Χριστὸν λαλεῖν καὶ ἰουδαΐζειν. ὁ γὰρ χριστιανισμὸς οὐκ εἰς Χριστιανισμόν, ᾧ πᾶσα γλῶσσα πιστεύσασα εἰς θεὸν συνήχθη.

## XI

1. Ταῦτα δέ, ἀγαπητοί μου, οὐκ ἐπεὶ ἔγνων τινὰς ἐξ ὑμῶν οὕτως ἔχοντας, ἀλλ' ὡς μικρότερος ὑμῶν ἄγκιστρα τῆς κενοδοξίας, ἀλλὰ πεπληροφορῆσθαι ἐν τῇ γεννήσει καὶ τῷ πάθει καὶ τῇ ἀναστάσει τῇ γενομένῃ ἐν καιρῷ τῆς ἡγεμονίας Ποντίου Πιλάτου· πραχθέντα ἀληθῶς καὶ βεβαίως ὑπὸ Ἰησοῦ Χριστοῦ, τῆς ἐλπίδος ἡμῶν, ἧς ἐκτραπῆναι μηδενὶ ὑμῶν γένοιτο.

## XII

1. Ὀναίμην ὑμῶν κατὰ πάντα, ἐάνπερ ἄξιος ὦ. εἰ γὰρ καὶ δέδεμαι, πρὸς ἕνα τῶν λελυμένων ὑμῶν ουκ εἰμί. οἶδα ὅτι οὐ φυσιοῦσθε· Ἰησοῦν γὰρ Χριστὸν ἔχετε ἐν ἑαυτοῖς· καὶ μᾶλλον, ὅταν ἐπαινῶ ὑμᾶς, οἶδα, ὅτι ἐντρέπεσθε, ὡς γέγραπται, ὅτι ὁ δίκαιος ἑαυτοῦ κατήγορος.

## XIII

1. Σπουδάζετε οὖν βεβαιωθῆναι ἐν τοῖς δόγμασιν τοῦ κυρίου καὶ τῶν ἀποστόλων, ἵνα πάντα, ὅσα ποιεῖτε, καευοδωθητε σαρκὶ καὶ πενεύματι, ἐν ἀρψῇ καὶ ἐν τέλει, μετὰ τοῦ ἀξιοπρεπεστάτου ἐπισκόπου ὑμῶν καὶ ἀξιοπλόκου πνευματικοῦ στεφάνου τοῦ πρεσβυτερίου ὑμῶν καὶ τῶν κατὰ θεὸν διακόνων. 2. ὑποτάγητε τῷ ἐπισκόπῳ καὶ ἀλλήλοις, ὡς Ἰησοῦς Χριστὸς τῷ πατρὶ καὶ οἱ ἀπόστολοι τῷ Χριστῷ καὶ τῷ πατρὶ ἵνα ἕνωσις ᾖ σαρκική τε καὶ πνευματική.

## XIV

1. Ἐιδώς, ὅτι θεοῦ γέμετε, συντόμως παρεκεπλευσα ὑμᾶς. μνημονεύετέ μου ἐν ταῖς προσευχαῖς ὑμῶν, ἵνα θεοῦ ἐπιτύχω, καὶ τῆς ἐν Συρίᾳ ἐκκλησίας, ὅθεν οὐκ ἄξιός εἰμι καλεῖσθαι· ἐπιδέομαι γὰρ τῆς ἡνωμένης ὑμῶν ἐν θεῷ προσευχῆς καὶ ἀγάπης, εἰς τὸ ἀξιωθῆναι τὴν ἐν Συρίᾳ ἐκκλησίαν διὰ τῆς ἐκκλησίας ὑμῶν δροσισθῆναι.

## XV

1. Ἀσπάζονται ὑμᾶς Ἐφέσιοι ἀπὸ Σμύρνης, ὅθεν και γράφω ὑμῖν, παρόντες εἰς δόξαν θεοῦ, ὥσπερ καὶ ὑμεῖσ οἳ κατὰ πάντα με ἀνέπαυσαν ἅμα Πολυκάρπῳ, ἐπισκόπῳ Σμυρναίων. καὶ αἱ λοιπαὶ δὲ ἐκκλησίαι ἐν τιμῇ Ἰησοῦ Χριστοῦ ἀσπάσονται ὑμᾶς. ἔρρωσθε ἐν ὁμονοίᾳ θεοῦ, κεκτημένοι ἀδιάκριτον πνεῦμα, ὅς ἐστιν Ἰησοῦς Χριστός.

# The Epistle of Ignatius to the Trallians

## Chapter. Prologue

Ignatius, who is also Theophorus, unto her that is beloved by God the Father of Jesus Christ; to the holy church which is in Tralles of Asia, elect and worthy of God, having peace in flesh and spirit through the passion of Jesus Christ, who is our hope through our resurrection unto Him; which church also I salute in the Divine plenitude after the apostolic fashion, and I wish her abundant greeting.

## Chapter. 1

I have learned that ye have a mind unblamable and steadfast in patience, not from habit, but by nature, according as Polybius your bishop informed me, who by the will of God and of Jesus Christ visited me in Smyrna; and so greatly did he rejoice with me in my bonds in Christ Jesus, that in him I beheld the whole multitude of you.

Having therefore received your godly benevolence at his hands, I gave glory, forasmuch as I had found you to be imitators of God, even as I had learned.

## Chapter. 2

For when ye are obedient to the bishop as to Jesus Christ, it is evident to me that ye are living not after men but after Jesus Christ, who died for us, that believing on His death ye might escape death.

It is therefore necessary, even as your wont is, that ye should do nothing without the bishop; but be ye obedient also to the presbytery, as to the Apostles of Jesus Christ our hope; for if we live in Him, we shall also be found in Him.

And those likewise who are deacons of the mysteries of Jesus Christ must please all men in all ways. For they are not deacons of meats and drinks but servants of the Church of God. It is right therefore that they should beware of blame as of fire.

## Chapter. 3

In like manner let all men respect the deacons as Jesus Christ, even as they should respect the bishop as being a type of the Father and the presbyters as the council of God and as the college of Apostles. Apart from these there is not even the name of a church.

And I am persuaded that ye are so minded as touching these matters: for I received the ensample of your love, and I have it with me, in the person of your bishop, whose very demeanor is a great lesson, while his gentleness is power--a man to whom I think even the godless pay reverence.

Seeing that I love you I thus spare you, though I might write more sharply on his behalf: but I did not think myself competent for this, that being a convict I should order you as though I were an Apostle.

## Chapter. 4

I have many deep thoughts in God: but I take the measure of myself, lest I perish in my boasting. For now I ought to be the more afraid and not to give heed to those that would puff me up: for they that say these things to me are a scourge to me.

For though I desire to suffer, yet I know not whether I am worthy: for the envy of the devil is unseen indeed by many, but against me it wages the fiercer war. So then I crave gentleness, whereby the prince of this world is brought to nought.

## Chapter. 5

Am I not able to write to you of heavenly things? But I fear lest I should cause you harm being babes. So bear with me, lest not being able to take them in, ye should be choked.

For I myself also, albeit I am in bonds and can comprehend heavenly things and the arrays of the angels and the musterings of the principalities, things visible and things invisible---I myself am not yet by reason of this a disciple. For we lack many things, that God may not be lacking to us.

## Chapter. 6

I exhort you therefore-yet not I, but the love of Jesus Christ-take ye only Christian food, and abstain from strange herbage, which is heresy:

for these men do even mingle poison with Jesus Christ, imposing upon others by a show of honesty, like persons administering a deadly drug with honeyed wine, so that one who knoweth it not, fearing nothing, drinketh in death with a baneful delight.

## Chapter. 7

Be ye therefore on your guard against such men. And this will surely be, if ye be not puffed up and if ye be inseparable from [God] Jesus Christ and from the bishop and from the ordinances of the Apostles.

He that is within the sanctuary is clean; but he that is without the sanctuary is not clean, that is, he that doeth aught without the bishop and presbytery and deacons, this man is not clean in his conscience.

## Chapter. 8

Not indeed that I have known of any such thing among you, but I keep watch over you betimes, as my beloved, for I foresee the snares of the devil. Do ye therefore arm yourselves with gentleness and recover yourselves in faith which is the flesh of the Lord, and in love which is the blood of Jesus Christ.

Let none of you bear a grudge against his neighbor. Give no occasion to the Gentiles, lest by reason of a few foolish men the godly multitude be blasphemed: for Woe unto him through whom My name is vainly blasphemed before some.

## Chapter. 9

Be ye deaf therefore, when any man speaketh to you apart from Jesus Christ, who was of the race of David, who was the Son of Mary, who was truly born and ate and drank, was truly persecuted under Pontius Pilate, was truly crucified and died in the sight of those in heaven and those on earth and those under the earth;

who moreover was truly raised from the dead, His Father having raised Him, who in the like fashion will so raise us also who believe on Him--His Father, I say, will raise us--in Christ Jesus, apart from whom we have not true life.

## Chapter. 10

But if it were as certain persons who are godless, that is unbelievers, say, that He suffered only in semblance, being themselves mere semblance, why am I in bonds? And why also do I desire to fight with wild beasts? So I die in vain. Truly then I lie against the Lord.

## Chapter. 11

Shun ye therefore those vile offshoots that gender a deadly fruit, whereof if a man taste, forthwith he dieth. For these men are not the Father's planting:

for if they had been, they would have been seen to be branches of the Cross, and their fruit imperishable--the Cross whereby He through His passion inviteth us, being His members. Now it cannot be that a head should be found without members, seeing that God promiseth union, and this union is Himself

## Chapter. 12

I salute you from Smyrna, together with the churches of God that are present with me; men who refreshed me in all ways both in flesh and in spirit.

My bonds exhort you, which for Jesus Christ's sake I bear about, entreating that I may attain unto God; abide ye in your concord and in prayer one with another. For it becometh you severally, and more especially the presbyters, to cheer the soul of your bishop unto the honor of the Father [and to the honor] of Jesus Christ and of the Apostles.

I pray that ye may hearken unto me in love, lest I be for a testimony against you by having so written. And pray ye also for me who have need of your love in the mercy of God, that I may be vouchsafed the lot which I am eager to attain, to the end that I be not found reprobate.

## Chapter. 13

The love of the Smyrnaens and Ephesians saluteth you. Remember in your prayers the church which is in Syria; whereof [also] I am not worthy to be called a member, being the very last of them.

Fare ye well in Jesus Christ, submitting yourselves to the bishop as to the commandment, and likewise also to the presbytery; and each of you severally love one another with undivided heart.

My spirit is offered up for you, not only now, but also when I shall attain unto God. For I am still in peril; but the Father is faithful in Jesus Christ to fulfill my petition and yours. May we be found unblamable in Him.

# GREEK

## ΤΡΑΛΛΙΑΝΟΙΣ ΙΓΝΑΤΙΟΣ

Ἰγνάτιος, ὁ καὶ Θεοφόρος, ἠγαπημένῃ θεῷ, πατρι Ἰησοῦ Χριστοῦ, ἐκκλησίᾳ ἁγίᾳ τῇ οὔσῃ ἐν Τράλλεσιν τῆς Ἀσίας, ἐκλεκτῇ καὶ ἀξιοθέῳ, εἰρηνευούσῃ ἐν σαρκὶ καὶ πνεύματι τῷ πάθει Ἰησοῦ Χριστοῦ, τῆς ἐλπίδος ἡμῶν ἐν τῇ εἰς αὐτὸν ἀναστάσει· ἣν καὶ ἀσπάζομαι ἐν τῷ πληρώματι ἐν ἀποστολικῷ χαρακτῆρι καὶ εὔχομαι πλεῖστα χαίρειν.

### I

1. Ἄμωμον διάνοιαν καὶ αδιάκριτον ἐν ὑπομονῇ ἔγνων ὑμᾶς ἔχοντας, οὐ κατὰ χρῆσιν ἀλλὰ κατὰ φύσιν, καθὼς ἐδήλωσέν μοι Πολύβιος, ὁ ἐπίσκοπος ὑμῶν, ὃς παρεγένετο θελήματι θεοῦ καὶ Ἰησοῦ Χριστοῦ ἐν Σμύρνῃ καὶ οὕτως μοι συνεχάρη δεδεμένῳ ἐν Χριστῷ Ἰησοῦ, ὥστε με τὸ πᾶν πλῆθος ὑμῶν ἐν αὐτῷ θεωρεῖσθαι. 2. ἀποδεξάμενος οὖν τὴν κατὰ θεὸν εὔνοιαν δι᾽ αὐτοῦ εδόξασα, εὑρῶν ὑμᾶς, ὡς ἔγνων, μιμητὰς ὄντας θεοῦ.

### II

1. Ὅταν γὰρ τῷ ἐπισκόπῳ ὑοτάσσησθε ὡς Ἰησοῦ Χριστῷ, φαίνεσθέ μοι οὐ κατὰ ἄνθρωπον ζῶντες, ἀλλὰ κατὰ Ἰησοῦν Χριστὸν τὸν δι᾽ ἡμᾶς ἀποθανόντα, ἵνα πιστεύσαντες εἰς τὸν θάνατον αὐτοῦ τὸ ἀποθανεῖν ἐκφύγητε. 2. ἀναγκαῖον οὖν ἐστίν,

ὥσπερ ποιεῖτε, ἄνευ τοῦ ἐπισκόπου μηδὲν πράσσειν ὑμᾶς, ἀλλ' ὑποτάσσεσθαι καὶ τῷ πρεσβυτερίῳ ὡς τοῖς ἀποστόλοις Ἰησοῦ Χριστοῦ 3. δεῖ δὲ καὶ τοὺς διακόνους ὄντας μυστηρίων Ἰησοῦ Χριστοῦ κατὰ πάντα τρόπον πᾶσιν ἀρέσκειν. οὐ γὰρ βρωμάτων καὶ ποτῶν εἰσιν διάκονοι, ἀλλ' ἐκκλησίας θεοῦ ὑπηρέται· δέον οὖν αὐτοὺς φυλάσσεσθαι τὰ ἐγκλήματα ὡς πῦρ.

## III

1. Ὁμοίως πάντες ἐντρεπέσθωσαν τοὺς διακόνους ὡς Ἰησοῦν Χριστόν, ὡς καὶ τὸν ἐπίσκοπον ὄντα τύπον τοῦ πατρός, τοὺς δὲ πρεσβυτέρους ὡς συνέδριον θεοῦ καὶ ὡς σύνδεσμον ἀποστόλων. χωρὶς τούτων ἐκκλησία οὐ καλεῖται. 2. περὶ ὧν πέπεισμαι ὑμᾶς οὕτως ἔχειν. τὸ γὰρ ἐξεμπλάριον τῆς ἀγάπης ὑμῶν ἔλαβον καὶ ἔχω μεθ' ἑαυτοῦ ἐν τῷ ἐπισκόπῳ ὑμῶν, οὗ αὐτὸ τὸ κατάστημα μεγάλη μαθητεία, ἡ δὲ πραότης αὐτοῦ δύναμις· ὃν λογίζομαι καὶ τοὺς ἀθέους ἐντρέπεσθαι. 3. ἀγαπῶν ὑμᾶς φείδομαι, συντονώτερον δυνάμενος γράφειν ὑπὲρ τούτου. οὐκ εἰς τοῦτο ᾠήθην, ἵνα ὢν κατάκριτος ὡς ἀπόστολος ὑμῖν διατάσσωμαι.

## IV

1. Πολλὰ φρονῶ ἐν θεῷ, ἀλλ' ἐμαυτὸν μετρῶ, ἵνα μὴ ἐν καυχήσει απόλωμαι. νῦν γὰρ με δεῖ πλέον φοβεῖσθαι καὶ μὴ προσέχειν τοῖς φυσιοῦσίν με. οἱ γὰρ λέγοντές μοι μαστιγοῦσίν με. 2. ἀγαπῶ μὲν γὰρ τὸ παθεῖν, ἀλλ' οὐκ οἶδα, εἰ ἄξιός εἰμι. τὸ γὰρ ζῆλος πολλοῖς μὲν οὐ φαίνεται, ἐμὲ δὲ πλέον πολεμεῖ. χρῄζω οὖν πραότητος, ἐν ᾗ καταλύεται ὁ ἄρχων τοῦ αἰῶνος τούτου.

## V

1. Μὴ οὐ δύναμαι ὑμῖν τὰ ἐπουράνια γράψαι; ἀλλὰ φοβοῦμαι, μὴ νηπίοις οὖσιν ὑμῖν βλάβην παραθῶ· καὶ συγγνωμονεῖτέ μοι, μήποτε οὐ ἐγώ, οὐ καθότι δέδεμαι καὶ δύναμαι νοῖν τὰ ἐπουράνια καὶ τὰς τοποθεσίας τὰς ἀγγελικὰς καὶ τὰς συστάσεις τὰς ἀρχοντικάς, ὁρατά τε καὶ ἀόρατα, παρὰ τοῦτο ἤδη καὶ μαθητής εἰμι. πολλὰ γὰρ ἡμῖν λείπει, ἵνα θεοῦ μὴ λειπώμεθα.

## VI

1. Παρακαλῶ οὖν ὑμᾶς, οὐκ ἐγώ, ἀλλ᾽ ἡ ἀγάπη Ἰησοῦ Χριστοῦ· μόνῃ τῇ χριστιανῇ τροφῇ χρῆσθε, ἀλλοτρίας δὲ βοτάνης ἀπέχεσθε, ἥτις ἐστὶν αἵρεσις· 2. οἳ ἑαυτοῖς παρεμπλέκουσιν Ἰησοῦν Χριστὸν καταξιοπιστευόμενοι, ὥσπερ θανάσιμον φάρμακον διδόντες μετὰ οἰνομέλιτος, ὅπερ ὁ ἀγνοῶν ἡδέως λαμβάνει ἐν ἡδονῇ κακῇ τὸ ἀποθανεῖν.

## VII

1. Φυλάττεσθε οὖν τοὺς τοιούτους. τοῦτο δὲ ἔσται ὑμῖν φυσιουμένοις καὶ οὖσιν ἀχωρίστοις θεοῦ Ἰησοῦ Χριστοῦ καί τοῦ ἐπισκόπου καὶ τῶν διαταγμάτων τῶν ἀποστόλων. 2. ὁ ἐντὸς θυσιαστηρίου ὢν καθαρός ἐστιν· τοῦτ᾽ ἔστιν, ὁ χωρὶς ἐπισκόπου καὶ πρεσβυτερίου καὶ διακόνων πράσσων τι, οὗτος καθαρός ἐστιν τῇ συνειδήσει.

## VIII

1. Οὐκ ἐπεὶ ἔγνων τοιοῦτόν τι ἐν ὑμῖν, ἀλλὰ προφυλάσσω ὑμᾶς ὄντας μου αθγαπητούς, προορῶν τὰς ἐνέδρας τοῦ διαβόλου, ὑμεῖς οὖ τὴν πραϋπάθειαν ἀναλαβόντες ἀνακτήσασθε ἑαυτοὺς

ἐν πίστει ὅ ἐστιν σὰρξ τοῦ κυρίου, καὶ ἐν ἀγάπῃ, ὅ ἐστιν αἷμα Ἰησοῦ Χριστοῦ. 2. μηδεὶς ὑμῶν κατὰ τοῦ πλησίον ἐχέτω. μὴ ἀφορμὰς δίδοτε τοῖς ἔθνεσιν, ἵνα μὴ δι' ὀλίγους ἄφρονας τὸ ἐν θεῷ πλῆθος βλασφημῆται. Οὐαὶ γάρ, δι' οὗ ἐπὶ ματαιότητι τὸ ὄνομά μου ἐπί τινων βλασφημεῖται.

## IX

1. Κωφώθητε οὖν, ὅταν ὑμῖν χωρὶς Ἰησοῦ Χριστοῦ λαλῇ τις, τοῦ ἐκ γένους Δαυείδ, τοῦ ἐκ Μαρίας, ὃς ἀληθῶς ἐγεννήθη, ἔφαγέν τε καὶ ἔπιεν, ἀληθῶς ἐδιώχθη ἐπὶ Ποντίου Πιλάτου, ἀληθῶς ἐσταυρώθη καὶ ἐπιγείων καὶ ὑποχθονίων. 2. ὃς καὶ ἀληθῶς ἠγέρθη ἀπό νεκρῶν, ἐγείραντος αὐτὸν τοῦ πατρὸς αὐτοῦ, κατὰ τὸ ὁμοίωμα ὃς καὶ ἡμᾶς τοὺς πιστεύοντας αὐτῷ οὕτως ἐγερεῖ ὁ πατὴρ αὐτοῦ ἐν Χριστῷ Ἰησοῦ, οὗ χωρὶς τὸ ἀληθινὸν ζῆν οὐκ ἔχομεν.

## X

1. Εἰ δέ, ὥσπερ τινὲς ἄθεοι ὄντες, τουτέστιν ἄπιστοί, λέγουσιν, τὸ δοκεῖν πεπονθέναι αὐτόν, αὐτοὶ ὄντες τὸ δοκεῖν, ἐγὼ τί δέδεμαι, τί δὲ καὶ εὔχομαι θηριομαχῆσαι; δωρεὰν οὖν ἀποθνήσκω. ἄρα οὖν καταψεύδομαι τοῦ κυρίου.

## XI

1. Φεύγετε οὖν τὰς κακὰς παραφυάδας τὰς γεννώσας καρπὸν

θανατηφόρον, οὗ ἐὰν γεύσηταί φυτεία πατρός. 2. εἰ γὰρ ἦσαν, ἐφαίνοντο ἂν κλάδοι τοῦ σταυροῦ, καὶ ἦν ἂν ὁ καρπὸς αὐτῶν ἄφθαρτος· δι' οὗ ἐν τῷ πάθει αὐτοῦ προσκαεῖται ὑμᾶς ὄντας μέλη αὐτοῦ. οὐ δύναται οὖν κεφαλὴ χωρὶς γεννηθῆναι ἄνευ μελῶν, τοῦ θεοῦ ἕνωσιν ἐπαγγελλομένου, ὅ ἐστιν αὐτός.

## XII

1. Ἀσπάζομαι ὑμᾶς ἀπὸ Σμύρνης ἅμα ταῖς συμπαρούσαις μοι ἐκκλυσίαις τοῦ θεοῦ, οἳ κατὰ πάντα με ἀνέπαυσαν σαρκί τε καὶ πνεύματι. 2. παρακαλεῖ ὑμᾶς τὰ δεσμά μου, ἃ ἕνεκεν Ἰησοῦ Χριστοῦ περιφέρω, αἰτούμενος θεοῦ ἐπιτυχεῖν· διαμένετε ἐν τῇ ὁμονοίᾳ ὑμῶν καὶ τῇ μετ' ἀλλήλων προσευχῇ. πρέπει γὰρ ὑμῖν τοῖς καθ' ἕνα, ἔξαιρέτως καὶ τοῖς πρεσβυτέροις, ἀναψύχειν τὸν ἐπισκοπον εἰς τιμὴν πατρός, Ἰησοῦ Χριστοῦ καὶ τῶν ἀποστόλων. 3. εὔχομαι ὑμᾶς ἐν ὑμῖν γράψας. καὶ περὶ ἐμοῦ δὲ προσεύχεσθε, τῆς ἀφ' τὸ καταξιωθῆναί με τοῦ κλήρου, οὗ περίκειμαι ἐπιτυχεῖν, ἵνα μὴ ἀδόκιμος εὑρεθῶ.

## XIII

1. Ἀσπάζεται ὑμᾶς ἡ ἀγάπη Σμυρναίων καὶ Ἐφεσίων. μνημονεύετε ἐν ταῖς προσευχαῖς ὑμῶν τῆς ἐν Συρίᾳ ἐκκλησίας, ὅθεν καὶ οὐκ ἄξιός εἰμι λέγεσθαι, ὢν ἔσχατος ἐκείνων. 2. ἔρρωσθε ἐν Ἰησοῦ Χριστῷ, ὑποτασσόμενοι τῷ ἐπισκόπῳ ὡς τῇ ἐντολῇ, ὁμοιως καὶ τῷ πρεσβυτερίῳ. καὶ οἱ κατ' ἄνδρα ἀλλήλους ἀγαπᾶτε ἐν ἀμερίστῳ καρδίᾳ. 3. ἁγνίζεται ὑμῶν τὸ ἐμὸν πνεῦμα οὐ μόνον νῦν, ἀλλὰ καὶ ὅταν θεοῦ ἐπιτύχω. ἔτι γὰρ ὑπὸ κίνδυνόν εἰμι· ἀλλὰ πιστὸς ὁ πατὴρ ἐν Ἰησοῦ Χριστῷ πληρῶσαί μου τὴν

αἴτησιν καὶ ὑμῶν, ἐν ᾧ εὑρεθείητε ἄμωμοι.

# The Epistle of Ignatius to the Romans

## Chapter. Prologue

Ignatius, who is also Theophorus, unto her that hath found mercy in the bountifulness of the Father Most High and of Jesus Christ His only Son; to the church that is beloved and enlightened through the will of Him who willed all things that are, by faith and love towards Jesus Christ our God; even unto her that hath the presidency in the country of the region of the Romans, being worthy of God, worthy of honor, worthy of felicitation, worthy of praise, worthy of success, worthy in purity, and having the presidency of love, walking in the law of Christ and bearing the Father's name; which church also I salute in the name of Jesus Christ the Son of the Father; unto them that in flesh and spirit are united unto His every commandment, being filled with the grace of God without wavering, and filtered clear from every foreign stain; abundant greeting in Jesus Christ our God in blamelessness.

## Chapter. 1

Forasmuch as in answer to my prayer to God it hath been granted me to see your godly countenances, so that I have obtained even more than I asked; for wearing bonds in Christ Jesus I hope to salute you, if it be the Divine will that I should be counted worthy to reach unto the end;

for the beginning verily is well ordered, if so be I shall attain unto the goal, that I may receive mine inheritance without hindrance. For I dread your very love, lest it do me an injury; for it is easy for you to do what ye will, but for me it is difficult to attain unto God, unless ye shall spare me.

## Chapter. 2

For I would not have you to be men-pleasers but to please God, as indeed ye do please Him. For neither shall I myself ever find an opportunity such as this to attain unto God, nor can ye, if ye be silent, win the credit of any nobler work. For, if ye be silent and leave me alone, I am a word of God; but if ye desire my flesh, then shall I be again a mere cry.

Nay grant me nothing more than that I be poured out a libation to God, while there is still an altar ready; that forming yourselves into a chorus in love ye may sing to the Father in Jesus Christ, for that God hath vouchsafed that the bishop from Syria should be found in the West, having summoned him from the East. It is good to set from the world unto God, that I may rise unto Him.

## Chapter. 3

Ye never grudged any one; ye were the instructors of others And my desire is that those lessons shall hold good which as teachers ye enjoin.

Only pray that I may have power within and without, so that I may not only say it but also desire it; that I may not only be called a Christian, but also be found one. For if I shall be found so, then can I also be called one, and be faithful then, when I am no more visible to the world.

Nothing visible is good. For our God Jesus Christ, being in the Father, is the more plainly visible. The Work is not of persuasiveness, but Christianity is a thing of might, whensoever it is hated by the world.

## Chapter. 4

I write to all the churches, and I bid all men know, that of my own free will I die for God unless Ye should hinder me. I exhort you, be ye not an unseasonable kindness to me. Let me be given to the wild beasts, for through them I can attain unto God. I am God's wheat, and I am ground by the teeth of wild beasts that I may be found pure bread [of Christ].

Rather entice the wild beasts, that they may become my sepulchre and may leave no part of my body behind, so that I may not, when I am fallen asleep, be burdensome to any one. Then shall I be truly a disciple of Jesus Christ, when the world shall not so much as see my body. Supplicate the Lord for me, that through these instruments I may be found a sacrifice to God.

I do not enjoin you, as Peter and Paul did. They were Apostles, I am a convict; they were free, but I am a slave to this very hour. Yet if I shall suffer, then am I a freed-man of Jesus Christ, and I shall rise free in Him. Now I am learning in my bonds to put away every desire.

## Chapter. 5

From Syria even unto Rome I fight with wild beasts, by land and sea, by night and by day, being bound amidst ten leopards, even a company of soldiers, who only wax worse when they are kindly treated. Howbeit through their wrong doings I become more completely a disciple; yet am I not hereby justified.

May I have joy of the beasts that have been prepared for me; and I pray that I may find them prompt; nay I will entice them that they may devour me promptly, not as they have done to some, refusing to touch them through fear. Yea though of themselves they should not be willing while I am ready, I myself will force them to it.

Bear with me. I know what is expedient for me. Now am I beginning to be a disciple. May naught of things visible and things invisible envy me; that I may attain unto Jesus Christ. Come fire and cross and grapplings with wild beasts, [cuttings and manglings,] wrenching of bones, hacking of limbs, crushings of my whole body, come cruel tortures of the devil to assail me. Only be it mine to attain unto Jesus Christ.

## Chapter. 6

The farthest bounds of the universe shall profit me nothing, neither the kingdoms of this world. It is good for me to die for Jesus Christ rather than to reign over the farthest bounds of the earth. Him I seek, who died on our behalf; Him I desire, who rose again [for our sake].

The pangs of a new birth are upon me. Bear with me, brethren. Do not hinder me from living; do not desire my death. Bestow not on the world one who desireth to be God's, neither allure him with material things. Suffer me to receive the pure light. When I am come thither, then shall I be a man.

Permit me to be an imitator of the passion of my God. If any man hath Him within himself, let him understand what I desire, and let him have fellow-feeling with me, for he knoweth the things which straiten me.

## Chapter. 7

The prince of this world would fain tear me in pieces and corrupt my mind to Godward. Let not any of you therefore who are near abet him. Rather stand ye on my side, that is on God's side. Speak not of Jesus Christ and withal desire the world. Let not envy have a home in you.

Even though I myself, when I am with you, should beseech you, obey me not; but rather give credence to these things which I write to you. [For] I write to you in the midst of life, yet lusting after death. My lust hath been crucified, and there is no fire of material longing in me, but only water living and speaking in me, saying within me, Come to the Father.

I have no delight in the food of corruption or in the delights of this life. I desire the bread of God, which is the flesh of Christ who was of the seed of David; and for a draught I desire His blood, which is love incorruptible.

## Chapter. 8

I desire no longer to live after the manner of men; and this shall be, if ye desire it. Desire ye, that ye yourselves also may be desired. In a brief letter I beseech you; believe me.

And Jesus Christ shall make manifest unto you these things, that I speak the truth--Jesus Christ, the unerring mouth in whom the Father hath spoken [truly].

Entreat ye for me, that I may attain [through the Holy Spirit]. I write not unto you after the flesh, but after the mind of God. If I shall suffer, it was your desire; if I shall be rejected, it was your hatred.

## Chapter. 9

Remember in your prayers the church which is in Syria, which hath God for its shepherd in my stead. Jesus Christ alone shall be its bishop-He and your love.

But for myself I am ashamed to be called one of them; for neither am I worthy, being the very last of them and an untimely birth: but I have found mercy that I should be some one, if so be I shall attain unto God.

My spirit saluteth you, and the love of the churches which received me in the name of Jesus Christ, not as a mere wayfarer; for even those churches which did not lie on my route after the flesh went before me from city to city.

## Chapter. 10

Now I write these things to you from Smyrna by the hand of the Ephesians who are worthy of all felicitation. And Crocus also, a name very dear to me, is with me, with many others besides.

As touching those who went before me from Syria to Rome unto the glory of God, I believe that ye have received instructions; whom also apprise that I am near; for they all are worthy of God and of you, and it becometh you to refresh them in all things.

These things I write to you on the ninth before the Calends of September. Fare ye well unto the end in the patient waiting for Jesus Christ.

# GREEK

# ΡΩΜΑΙΟΙΣ ΙΓΝΑΤΙΟΣ

Ἰγνάτιος, ὁ καὶ Θεοφόρος, τῇ ἠλεημένῃ ἐν μεγαλειότητι πατρὸς ὑψίστου καὶ Ἰησοῦ Χριστοῦ τοῦ μόνου υἱοῦ αὐτοῦ ἐκκλησίᾳ ἠγαπημένῃ καὶ πεφωτισμένῃ ἐν θελήματι τοῦ θελήσαντος τὰ πάντα, ἅ ἔστιν, κατὰ ἀγάπην Ἰησοῦ Χριστοῦ, τοῦ θεοῦ ἡμῶν, ἥτις καὶ προκάθηται ἐν τόπῳ χωρίου Ῥωμαίων, ἀξιόθεος, ἀξιεπίτευκτος, ἀξίαγνος καὶ προκαθημένη τῆς ἀγάπης, χριστώνυμος, πατρώνυμος, ἣν καὶ ἀσπάζομαι ἐν ὀνόματι Ἰησοῦ Χριστοῦ, υἱοῦ πατρός· κατὰ σάρκα καὶ πνεῦμα ἡνωμένοις πάσῃ ἐντολῇ αὐτοῦ, πεπληρωμένοις χάριτος θεοῦ ἀδιακρίτως καὶ ἀποδιϋλισμένοις ἀπὸ παντὸς ἀλλοτρίου χρώματος πλεῖστα ἐν Ἰησοῦ Χριστῷ, τῷ θεῷ ἡμῶν, ἀμώμως χαίρειν.

## I

1. Ἐπεὶ εὐξάμενος θεῷ ἐπέτυχον ἰδεῖν ὑμῶν τὰ ἀξιόθεα πρόσωπα, ὡς καὶ πλέον ᾐτούμην λαβεῖν· δεδεμένος γὰρ ἐν Χριστῷ Ἰησοῦ ἐλπίζω ὑμᾶς ἀσπάσμένος ἐάνπερ θέλημα ᾖ τοῦ ἀξιωθῆναί με εἰς τέλος εἶναι. 2. ἡ μὲν γὰρ ἀρχὴ εὐοικονόμητός ἐστιν, ἐάνπερ χάριτος ἐπιτύχω εἰς τὸ τὸν κλῆρόν μου ἀνεμποδίστως ἀπολαβεῖν. φοβοῦμαι γὰρ τὴν ὑμῶν ἀγάπην, μὴ αὐτή με ἀδικήσῃ. ὑμῖν γὰρ εὐχερές ἐστιν, ὃ θέλετε, ποιῆσαι· ἐμοὶ δὲ δύσκολόν ἐστιν τοῦ θεοῦ ἐπιτυχεῖν, ἐάνπερ ὑμεῖς μὴ φείσησθέ μου.

## II

1. Οὐ γὰρ θέλω ὑμᾶς ἀνθρωπαρεσκῆσαι, ἀλλὰ θεῷ ἀρέσαι,

ὥσπερ καὶ ἀρέκετε. οὔτε γὰρ ἐγώ ποτε ἕξω καιρὸν τοιοῦτον θεοῦ ἐπιτυχεῖν, οὔτε ὑμεῖς, ἐὰν σιωπήσητε, κρείττονι ἔργῳ ἔχετε ἐπιγραφῆναι. ἐὰν γὰρ σιωπήσητε ἀπ' ἐμοῦ, ἐγὼ λόγος θεοῦ· ἐὰν δὲ ἐρασθῆτε τῆς σαρκός μου, πάλιν ἔσομαι φωνή. 2. πλέον μοι μὴ παράσψησθε τοῦ σπονδισθῆναι θεῷ, ὡς ἔτι θυσιαστήριον ἕτοιμόν ἐστιν, ἵνα ἐν ἀγάπῃ χορὸς γενόμενοι ᾄσητε τῷ πατρὶ ἐν Χριστῷ Ἰησοῦ, ὅτι τὸν ἐπίσκοπον Συρίας ὁ θεὸς κατηξίωσεν εὑρεθῆναι εἰς δύσιν ἀπὸ ἀνατολῆς μεταπεμψάμενος. καλὸν τὸ δῦναι ἀπὸ κόσμου πρὸς θεόν, ἵνα εἰς αὐτὸν ἀνατείλω.

## III

1. Οὐδέποτε ἐβασκάνατε οὐδενί, ἄλλους ἐδιδάξατε. ἐγὼ δὲ θέλω, ἵνα κἀκεῖνα βέβαια ᾖ ἃ μαθητεύοντες ἐντέλλεσθε. 2. μόνον μοι δύναμιν αἰτεῖσθε ἔσωθέν τε καὶ ἐσωθέν τε καὶ ἔξωθεν, ἵνα μὴ μόνον λέγω ἀλλὰ καὶ θέλω, ἵνα μὴ μόνον λέγωμαι Χριστιανὸς ἀλλὰ καὶ εὑρεθῶ. ἐὰν γὰρ εὑρεθῶ, καὶ λέγεσθαι δύναμαι, καὶ τότε πιστὸς εἶναι, ὅταν κόσμῳ μὴ φαίνωμαι. 3. οὐδὲν φαινόμενον καλόν· ὁ γὰρ θεὸς ἡμῶν Ἰησοῦς Χριστὸς ἐν πατρὶ ὢν μᾶλλον φαίνεται. οὐ περσμονῆς τὸ ἔργον, ἀλλὰ μεγέθους ἐστὶν ὁ Χριστιανισμός, ὅταν μισῆται ὑπὸ κόσμου.

## IV

1. Ἐγὼ γράφω πάσαις ταῖς ἐκκλησίαις, καὶ ἐντέλλομαι πᾶσιν, ὅτι ἐγὼ ἑκὼν ὑπὲρ θεοῦ ἀποθνήσκω, ἐάνπερ ὑμεῖς μὴ κωλύσητε. παρακαλῶ ὑμᾶς, μὴ εὔνοια ἄκαιρος γένησθέ μοι. ἄφετέ με θηρίων εἶναι βοράν, δι' ὧν ἔνεστιν θεοῦ ἐπιτυχεῖν. σῖτός εἰμι θεοῦ καὶ δι' ὀδόντων θηρίων ἀλήθομαι, ἵνα καθαρὸς ἄρτος εὑρεθῶ τοῦ Χριστοῦ. 2. μᾶλλον κολκεύσαε τὰ θηρία, ἵνα μοι τάφος γένωνται καὶ μηδεν καταλίπωσι τῶν τοῦ σώματός μου, ἵνα μὴ κοιμηθεὶς

βαρὺς τινι γένωμαι. τότε ἔσομαι μαθητὴς ἀληθῶς Ἰησοῦ Χριστοῦ, ὅτε οὐδὲ τὸ σῶμα μου ὁ κόσμος ὄψεται. λιτανεύσατε τὸν Χριστὸν ὑπὲρ ἐμοῦ, ἵνα διὰ τῶν ὀργάνων τούτων θυσία εὑρεθῶ. 3. οὐχ ὡς Πέτρος καὶ Παῦλος διατάσσομαι ὑμῖν. ἐκεῖνοι ἀπόστολοι, ἐγὼ κατάκριτος· ἐκεῖνοι ἐλεύθεροι, ἐγώ δέ μέχρι νῦν δοῦλος. ἀλλ' ἐὰν πάθω, ἀπελεύθερος γενήσομαι Ἰησοῦ Χριστοῦ καὶ ἀναστήσομαι ἐν αὐτῷ ἐλεύθερος. νῦν μανθάνω δεδεμένος μηδὲν ἐπιθυμεῖν.

## V

1. Ἀπὸ Συρίας μέχρι Ῥώμης θηριομαχῶ, διὰ γῆς καὶ θαλάσσης, νυκτὸς καὶ ἡμέρας, δεδεμένος δέκα λεοπάρδοις, ὅ ἐστιν στρατιωτικὸν τάγμα· οἳ ἀδικήμασιν αὐτῶν μᾶλλον μαθητεύομαι, ἀλλ' οὐ παρὰ τοῦτο δεδικαίωμαι. 2. ὀναίμην τῶν θηρίων τῶν ἐμοὶ ἡτοιμασμένων καὶ εὔχομαι σύτομά μοι εὑρέθῆναι· ἃ καὶ κολακεύσω, συντόμως με καταφαγεῖν, οὐχ ὥσπερ τινῶν δειλαινόμενα οὐχ ἥψαντο. κἂν αὐτὰ δὲ ἄκοντα μη θελήσῃ, ἐγὼ προσβιάσομαι. 3. συγγνώμην μοι ἔχετε· τί μοι συμφέρει, ἐγὼ γινώσκω, νῦν ἄρχομαι μαθητὴς εἶναι, μηθέν με ζηλώσαι τῶν ὁρατῶν, ἵνα Ἰησοῦ Χριστοῦ ἐπιτύχω. πῦρ καὶ σταυρὸς θηρίων τε συστάσεις, ἀνατομαί, διαιρέσεις, σκρπισμοὶ ὀστέων, συγκοπὴ μελῶν, ἀλεσμοὶ ὅλου τοῦ σώματος, κακαὶ κολάσεις τοῦ διαβόλου ἐπ' ἐμὲ ἐρχέσθωσαν, μόνον ἵνα Ἰησοῦ Χριστοῦ ἐπιτύχω.

## VI

1. Οὐδέν μοι ὠφελήσει τὰ πέρατα τοῦ κόσμου οὐδὲ αἱ βασιλεῖαι τοῦ αἰῶνος τούτου. καλόν μοι ἀποθανεῖν εἰς Χριστὸν Ἰησοῦν, ἢ βασιλεύειν τῶν περάτων τῆς γῆς. ἐκεῖνον ζητῶ, τὸν ὑπὲρ ἡμῶν ἀποθανόντα· ἐκεῖνον θέλω, τὸν δι' ἡμᾶς ἀναστάντα. ὁ δὲ

τοκετός μοι ἐπίκειται. 2. σύγγνωτέ μοι, αδελφοί· μὴ ἐμποδίσηέ μοι ζῆσαι, μὴ θελήσητέ με ἀποθανεῖν· τὸν τοῦ θεοῦ θέλοντα εἶναι κόσμῳ μὴ χαρίσησθε, μηδὲ ὕλῃ ἐξαπατήσητε· ἄφετέ με καθαρὸν φῶς λαβεῖν· ἐκεῖ παραγενόμενος ἄνθρωπος ἔσομαι. 3. ἐπιτρέψατέ μοι μιμητὴν εἶναι του πάθους τοῦ θεοῦ μου. εἴ τις αὐτὸν ἐν ἑαυτῷ ἔχει, νοησάτω ὃ θέλω, καὶ συμπαθείτω μοι εἰδὼς τὰ συνέχοντά με.

## VII

1. Ὁ ἄρχων τοῦ αἰῶνος τούτου διαρπάσαι με βούλεται καὶ τὴν εἰς θεόν μου γνώμην διαφθεῖραι. μηδεὶς οὖν τῶν παρόντων ὑμῶν βοηθείτω αὐτῷ· μᾶλλον ἐμοῦ γίνεσθε, τουτέστιν τοῦ θεοῦ. μὴ λαλεῖτε Ἰησοῦν Χριστόν, κόσμον δὲ ἐπιθυμεῖτε. 2. βασκανία ἐν ὑμῖν μὴ κατοικείτω. μηδ' ἂν ἐγὼ παρὼν παρακαλῶ ὑμᾶς, πεισθητέ μοι· τούτοις δὲ μᾶλλον πείσθητε, οἷς γράφω ὑμῖν. ζῶν γὰρ ἐσταύρωται, καὶ οὐκ ἔστιν ἐν ἐμοὶ πῦρ φιλούλον· Δεῦρο πρὸς τὸν πατέρα. 3. οὐχ ἥδομαι τροφῇ θέλω, ὅ ἐστιν σὰρξ Ἰησοῦ Χριστοῦ τοῦ ἐκ σπέρματος Δαυείδ, καὶ πόμα θέλω τὸ αἷμα αὐτοῦ, ὅ ἐστιν ἀγάπη ἄφθαρτος.

## VIII

1. Οὐκέτι θέλω κατὰ ἀνθρώπους ζῆν. τοῦτο δέ ἔσται, ἐὰν ὑμεῖς θελήσητε. θελήσαε, ἵνα καὶ ὑμεῖς θεληθῆτε. 2. δι' ὀλίγων γραμμάτων αἰτοῦμαι ὑμᾶς· πιστεύσατέ μοι. Ἰησοῦς δὲ Χριστὸς ὑμῖν ταῦτα φανερώσει, ὅτι ἀληθῶς λέγων· τὸ ἀψευδὲσ στόμα, ἐν ᾧ ὁ πατὴρ ἐλάλησεν ἀληθῶς. 3. αἰτήσασθε περί ἐμοῦ, ἵνα ἐπιτύχω. οὐ κατὰ σάρκα ὑμῖν ἔγραψα, ἀλλὰ κατὰ γνωμην θεοῦ. ἐὰν πάθω, ἠθελήσατε· ἐὰν ἀποδοκιμασθῶ, ἐμισήσατε.

## IX

1. Μνημονεύετε ἐν τῇ προσευχῇ ὑμῶν τῆς ἐν Συρίᾳ ἐκκλησίας, ἥτις ἀντὶ ἐμοῦ ποιμένι τῷ θεῷ χρῆται. μόνος αὐτὴν Ἰησοῦς Χριστὸς ἐπισκοπήσει καὶ ἡ ὑμῶν ἀγάπη. 2. ἐγὼ δὲ αἰσχύνομαι ἐξ αὐτῶν καὶ ἔκτρωμα· ἀλλ' ἠλέημαί τις εἶναι, ἐὰν θεοῦ ἐπιτύχω. 3. ἀσπάζεται ὑμᾶς τὸ ἐμὸν πνεῦμα καὶ ἡ ἀγάπη τῶν ἐκκλησιῶν τῶν δεξαμένων με εἰς ὄνομα Ἰησοῦ Χριστοῦ, οὐχ ὡς παροδεύοντα. καὶ γὰρ αἱ μὴ προσήκουσαί μοι τῇ ὁδῷ τῇ κατὰ σάρκα, κατὰ πόλιν με προῆγον.

## X

1. Γράφω δὲ ὑμῖν ταῦτα ἀπὸ Σμύρνης δι' Ἐφεσίων τῶν ἀξιομακαρίστων. ἔστιν δὲ καὶ ἅμα ἐμοὶ σὺν πολλοῖς καὶ Κρόκος, τὸ ποθητόν μοι ὄνομα. 2. περὶ τῶν προελθόντων με ἀπὸ Συρίας εἰς Ῥώμην εἰς δόξαν τοῦ θεοῦ πιστεύω ὑμᾶς ἐπεγνωκέναι, οἷς καὶ δηλώσατε ἐγγύς με ὄντα. πάντες γάρ εἰσιν ἄξιοι τοῦ θεοῦ καὶ ὑμῶν· οὓς πρέπον ὑμῖν ταῦτα τῇ πρὸ ἐννέα καλανδῶν Σεπτεμβρίων. ἔρρωσθε εἰς τέλος ἐν ὑπομονῇ Ἰησοῦ Χριστοῦ.

# The Epistle of Ignatius to the Philadelphians

## Chapter. Prologue

Ignatius, who is also Theophorus, to the church of God the Father and of Jesus Christ, which is in Philadelphia of Asia which hath found mercy and is firmly established in the concord of God and rejoiceth in the passion of our Lord and in His resurrection without wavering, being fully assured in all mercy; which church I salute in the blood of Jesus Christ, that is eternal and abiding joy more especially if they be at one with the bishop and the presbyters who are with him, and with the deacons that have been appointed according to the mind of Jesus Christ, whom after His own will He confirmed and established by His Holy Spirit.

## Chapter. 1

This your bishop I have found to hold the ministry which pertaineth to the common weal, not of himself or through men, nor yet for vain glory, but in the love of God the Father and the Lord Jesus Christ. And I am amazed at his forbearance;

whose silence is more powerful than others speech. For he is attuned in harmony with the commandments, as a lyre with its strings. Wherefore my soul blesseth his godly mind, for I have found that it is virtuous and perfect--even the imperturbable and calm temper which he hath, while living in all godly forbearance.

## Chapter. 2

As children therefore [of the light] of the truth, shun division and wrong doctrines; and where the shepherd is, there follow ye as sheep.

For many specious wolves with baneful delights lead captive the runners in God's race; but, where ye are at one, they will find no place.

## Chapter. 3

Abstain from noxious herbs, which are not the husbandry of Jesus Christ, because they are not the planting of the Father. Not that I have found division among you, but filtering.

For as many as are of God and of Jesus Christ, they are with the bishop; and as many as shall repent and enter into the unity of the Church, these also shall be of God, that they may be living after Jesus Christ. Be not deceived, my brethren.

If any man followeth one that maketh a schism, he doth not inherit the kingdom of God. If any man walketh in strange doctrine, he hath no fellowship with the passion.

## Chapter. 4

Be ye careful therefore to observe one eucharist (for there is one flesh of our Lord Jesus Christ and one cup unto union in His blood; there is one altar, as there is one bishop, together with the presbytery and the deacons my fellow-servants), that whatsoever ye do, ye may do it after God.

## Chapter. 5

My brethren, my heart overfloweth altogether in love towards you; and rejoicing above measure I watch over your safety; yet not I, but Jesus Christ, wearing whose bonds I am the more afraid, because I am not yet perfected. But your prayer will make me perfect [unto God], that I may attain unto the inheritance wherein I have found mercy, taking refuge in the Gospel as the flesh of Jesus and in the Apostles as the presbytery of the Church.

Yea, and we love the prophets also, because they too pointed to the Gospel in their preaching and set their hope on Him and awaited Him; in whom also having faith they were saved in the unity of Jesus Christ, being worthy of all love and admiration as holy men, approved of Jesus Christ and numbered together in the Gospel of our common hope.

## Chapter. 6

But if any one propound Judaism unto you, hear him not: for it is better to hear Christianity from a man who is circumcised than Judaism from one uncircumcised. But if either the one or the other speak not concerning Jesus Christ, I look on them as tombstones and graves of the dead, whereon are inscribed only the names of men.

Shun ye therefore the wicked arts and plottings of the prince of this world, lest haply ye be crushed by his devices, and wax weak in your love. But assemble yourselves all together with undivided heart. And

I give thanks to my God, that I have a good conscience in my dealings with you, and no man can boast either in secret or openly, that I was burdensome to any one in small things or in great. Yea and for all among whom I spoke, it is my prayer that they may not turn it into a testimony against themselves.

## Chapter. 7

For even though certain persons desired to deceive me after the flesh, yet the spirit is not deceived, being from God; for it knoweth whence it cometh and whence it goeth, and it searcheth out the hidden things. I cried out, when I was among you; I spake with a loud voice, with God's own voice, Give ye heed to the bishop and the presbytery and deacons.

Howbeit there were those who suspected me of saying this, because I knew beforehand of the division of certain persons. But He in whom I am bound is my witness that I learned it not from flesh of man; it was the preaching of the Spirit who spake on this wise; Do nothing without the bishop; keep your flesh as a temple of God; cherish union; shun divisions; be imitators of Jesus Christ, as He Himself also was of His Father.

## Chapter. 8

I therefore did my own part, as a man composed unto union. But where there is division and anger, there God abideth not. Now the Lord forgiveth all men when they repent, if repenting they return to the unity of God and to the council of the bishop. I have faith in the grace of Jesus Christ, who shall strike off every fetter from you; and I entreat you,

Do ye nothing in a spirit of factiousness but after the teaching of Christ. For I heard certain persons saying, If I find it not in the charters, I believe it not in the Gospel. And when I said to them, It is written, they answered me That is the question. But as for me, my charter is Jesus Christ, the inviolable charter is His cross and His death and His resurrection, and faith through Him; wherein I desire to be justified through your prayers.

## Chapter. 9

The priests likewise were good, but better is the High-priest to whom is committed the holy of holies; for to Him alone are committed the hidden things of God; He Himself being the door of the Father, through which Abraham and Isaac and Jacob enter in, and the Prophets and the Apostles and the whole Church; all these things combine in the unity of God.

But the Gospel hath a singular preeminence in the advent of the Savior, even our Lord Jesus Christ, and His passion and resurrection. For the beloved Prophets in their preaching pointed to Him; but the Gospel is the completion of immortality. All things together are good, if ye believe through love.

## Chapter. 10

Seeing that in answer to your prayer and to the tender sympathy which ye have in Christ Jesus, it hath been reported to me that the church which is in Antioch of Syria hath peace, it is becoming for you, as a church of God, to appoint a deacon to go thither as God's ambassador, that he may congratulate them when they are assembled together, and may glorify the Name.

Blessed in Jesus Christ is he that shall be counted worthy of such a ministration; and ye yourselves shall be glorified. Now if ye desire it, it is not impossible for you to do this for the name of God; even as the churches which are nearest have sent bishops, and others presbyters and deacons.

## Chapter. 11

But as touching Philo the deacon from Cilicia, a man of good report, who now also ministereth to me in the word of God, together with Rhaius Agathopus, an elect one who followeth me from Syria, having bidden farewell to this present life; the same who also bear witness to you--and I myself thank God on your behalf, because ye received them, as I trust the Lord will receive you. But may those who treated them with dishonor be redeemed through the grace of Jesus Christ.

The love of the brethren which are in Troas saluteth you; from whence also I write to you by the hand of Burrhus, who was sent with me by the Ephesians and Smyrnaeans as a mark of honor. The Lord shall honor them, even Jesus Christ, on whom their hope is set in flesh and soul and spirit, by faith, love, and by concord. Fare ye well in Christ Jesus our common hope.

# GREEK

# ΦΙΛΑΔΕΛΦΕΥΣΙΝ ΙΓΝΑΤΙΟΣ

Ἰγνάτιος, ὁ καὶ Θεοφόρος, ἐκκλησίᾳ θεοῦ πατρὸς καὶ κυρίου Ἰησοῦ Χριστοῦ τῇ οὔσῃ ἐν Φιλαδελφίᾳ τῆς Ἀσίας, ἠλεημένῃ καὶ ἡδρασμένῃ ἐν ὁμονοίᾳ θεοῦ καὶ ἀγαλλιωμένῃ ἐν τῷ πάθει τοῦ κυρίου ἡμῶν ἀδιακρίτως καὶ ἐν τῇ ἀναστάσει αὐτοῦ πεπληροφορημένῃ ἐν παντὶ ελέει, ἣν ἀσπάζομαι ἐν αἵματι Ἰησοῦ Χριστοῦ, ἥτις ἐστὶν χαρὰ αἰώνιος καὶ παράμονος, μάλιστα ἐὰν ἐν ἑνὶ ὦσιν σὺν τῷ ἐπισκόπῳ καὶ τοῖς σὺν αὐτῳ πρεσβυτέροις καὶ διακόνοις ἀποδεδειγμένοις ἐν γνώμῃ Ἰησοῦ Χριστοῦ, οὓς κατὰ τὸ ἴδιον θέλημα ἐστήριξεν ἐν βεβαιωσύνῃ τῷ ἁγίῳ αὐτοῦ πνεύματι.

## I

1. Ὃν ἐπίσκοπον ἔγνων οὐκ ἀφ' ἑαυτοῦ οὐδὲ δι' ἀνθρώπων κεκτῆσθαι τὴν διακονίαν τὴν εἰς τὸ κοινὸν ἀνήδουσαν οὐδὲ κατὰ κενοδοξίαν, ἀλλ' ἐν ἀγαπῃ θεοῦ πατρὸς καὶ κυρίου Ἰησοῦ Χριστοῦ· οὗ καταπέπληγμαι τὴν ἐπιείκειαν, ὃς σιγῶν πλείονα δύαται τῶν μάταια λαλούντων. 2. συνευρυθμισται γὰρ ταῖς ἐντολας ὡς χορδαῖς κιθάρα. διὸ μακαρίζει μου ἡ ψυχὴ τὴν εἰς θεὸν αὐτοῦ γνώμην, ε0πιγνοὺς ἐνάρετον καὶ τέλειον οὖσαν, τὸ ἀκίνητον αὐτοῦ καὶ τὸ ἀόργητον αὐτου ἐν πάσῃ ἐπιεικείᾳ θεοῦ ζῶντος.

## II

1. Τέκνα οὖν φωτὸς ἀληθείας, φεύγετε τὸν μερισμὸν καὶ τὰς κακοδιδασκαλίας· ὅπου δὲ ὁ ποιμὴν ἐστιν, ἐκεῖ ὡς πρόβατα ἀκολουθεῖτε. 2. πολλοὶ γὰρ λύκοι ἀξιόπιστοι ἡδονῇ κακῇ

αἰχμαλωτίζουσιν τοὺς θεοδρόμους· ἀλλ' ἐν τῇ ἑνότητι ὑμῶν οὐχ ἕξουσιν τόπον.

## III

1. Ἀπέχεσθε τῶν κακῶν βοτανῶν, ἅτινας οὐ γεωργεῖ Ἰησοῦς Χριστός, διὰ τὸ μὴ εἶναι αὐτοὺς φυτείαν πατρός· οὐχ ὅτι παρ' ὑμῖν μερισμὸν εὗρον, ἀλλ' ἀποδιυλισμόν. 2. ὅσοι γὰρ θεοῦ εἰσιν καὶ Ἰησοῦ Χριστοῦ, οὗτοι μετὰ τοῦ ἐπισκόπου εἰσίν. καὶ ὅσοι ἂν μεταμοήσαντες ἔλθωσιν ἐπὶ τὴν ἑνότητα τῆς ἐκκλησίας, καὶ οὗτοι θεοῦ ἔσονται, ἵνα ὦσιν κατὰ Ἰησοῦν Χριστὸν ζῶντες. 3. μὴ πλανᾶσθε, ἀδελφοί μου· εἴ τις σχίζοντι ἀκολουθεῖ, βασιλείαν θεοῦ οὐ κληρονομεῖ· εἴ τις ἐν ἀλλοτρίᾳ γνώμῃ περιπατεῖ, οὗτος τῷ πάθει οὐ συγκατατίθεται.

## IV

Σπουδάσατε οὖν μιᾷ εὐχαριστίᾳ χρῆσθαι· μία γὰρ σὰρξ τοῦ κυρίου ἡμῶν Ἰηςοῦ Χριστοῦ καὶ ἓν ποτήριον εἰς ἕωσιν τοῦ αἵματος αὐτοῦ, ἓν θυσιαστήριον, ὡς εἷς ἐπίσκοπος ἅμα τῷ πρεσβυτερίῳ καὶ διακόνοις τοῖς συνδούλοις μου· ἵνα, ὁ ἐὰν πράσσητε, κατὰ θεὸν πράσσητε.

## V

1.Ἀδελφοίμου,λίανἐκκέχυμαιἀγαπῶνὑμᾶςκαὶὑπεραγαλλόμενος ἀσφαλίζομαι ὑμᾶς· οὐκ ἐγὼ δέ, ἀλλ' Ἰησοῦς Χριστός, ἐν ᾧ δεδεμένος φοβοῦμαι μᾶλλον, ὡς ἔτι ὢν ἀναπάρτιστος· ἀλλ' ἡ προσευχὴ ὑμῶν εἰς θεόν με ἀπαρτίσει, ἵνα ἐν ᾧ κλήρῳ ἠλεήθην ἐπιτύχω, προσφυγὼν τῷ εὐαγγελίῳ ὡς σαρκὶ Ἰησοῦ, καὶ τοῖς ἀποστόλοις ὡς πρεσβυτερίῳ ἐκκλησίας. 2. καὶ τοὺς προφήτας δὲ ἀγαπῶμεν, διὰ τὸ καὶ αὐτοὺς εἰς τὸ εὐαγγέλιον κατηγγελκέναι καὶ εἰς αὐτὸν ἐλπίζειν καὶ αὐτὸν ἀναμένειν, ἐν ᾧ καὶ πιστεύσαντες ἐσώθησαν, ἐν ἑνότητι Ἰησοῦ Χριστοῦ ὄντες, ἀξιαγάπητοι καὶ ἀξιοθαύμαστοι ἅγιοι, ὑπὸ Ἰησοῦ Χριστοῦ μεμαρτυρημένοι καὶ συνηριθμημένοι ἐν τῷ εὐαγγελίῳ τῆς κοινῆς ἐλπίδος.

## VI

1. Ἐὰν δέ τις ἰουδαϊσμὸν ἑρμηνεύῃ ὑμῖν, μὴ ἀκούετε αὐτοῦ. ἄμεινον γάρ ἐστιν παρὰ ἀδρὸς περιτομὴν ἔχοντος χριστιανισμὸν ἀκούειν, ἢ παρὰ ἀκροβύστου ἰουδαϊσμόν. ἐὰν δὲ ἀμφότεροι περὶ Ἰησοῦ Χριστοῦ μὴ λαλῶσιν, οὗτοι ἐμοὶ στῆλαι εἰσιν καὶ τάφοι νεκρῶν, ἐφ' οἷς γέγραπται μόνον ὀνόματα ἀνθρώπων. 2. φεύγετε οὖν τὰς κακοτεχνίας καὶ ἐνέδρας τοῦ ἄρχοντος τοῦ αἰῶνος τούτου, μήποτε θλιβέντες τῇ γνώμῃ αὐτοῦ ἐξασθενήσετε ἐν τῇ ἀγάπῃ· ἀλλὰ πάντες ἐπὶ τὸ αὐτὸ γίνεσθε ἐν ἀμερίστῳ καρδίᾳ. 3. εὐχαριστῶ δὲ τῷ θεῷ μου, ὅτι εὐσυνείδητός εἰμι ἐν ὑμῖν καὶ οὐκ ἔχει τις καυχήσασθαι οὔτε λάθρα οὔτε φανερῶς, ὅτι ἐβάρησά τινα ἐν μικρῷ ἢ ἐν μεγάλῳ. καὶ πᾶσι δέ, ἐν οἷς ἐλάλησα, εὔχομαι, ἵνα μὴ εἰς μαρτύριον αὐτὸ κτήσωνται.

## VII

1. Εἰ γὰρ καὶ κατὰ σάρκα μέ τινες ἠθέλησαν πλανῆσαι, ἀλλὰ τὸ πνεῦμα οὐ πλανᾶται ἀπὸ θεοῦ ὄν. οἶδεν γάρ, πόθεν ἔρχεται καὶ ποῦ ὑπάγει, καὶ τὰ κρυπτὰ ἐλέγχει. ἐκραύγασα μεταξὺ ὤν, ἐλάλουν μεγάλῃ φωνῇ, θεοῦ φωνῇ· Τῷ ἐπισκόπῳ προσέχετε καὶ τῷ πρεσβυτερίῳ καὶ διανόνοις. 2. οἱ δὲ ὑποπτεύσαντές με ὡς πρειδότα τὸν μερισμόν τινων λέγειν ταυτα· μάρτυς δέ μοι, ἐν ᾧ δέδεμαι, ὅτι ἀπὸ σαρκὸς ἀνθρωπίνης οὐκ ἔγνων. τὸ δὲ πνεῦμα

ἐκήρυσσεν λέγον τάδε· Χωρις τοῦ ἐπισκόπου μηδὲν ποιεῖτε, τὴν σάρκα ὑμῶν ὡς ναὸν θεοῦ τηρεῖτε, τὴν ἕνωσιν ἀγαπᾶτε, τοὺς μερισμοὺς φεύγετε, μιμηταὶ γίνεσθε Ἰησοῦ Χριστοῦ, ὡς καὶ αὐτὸς τοῦ πατρὸς αὐτοῦ.

## VIII

1. Ἐγὼ μὲν οὖν τὸ ἴδιον ἐποίουν ὡς ἄνθρωπος εἰς ἕνωσιν κατηρτισμένος. οὗ δὲ μερισμός ἐστιν και ὀργῄ, θεὸς οὐ καοικεῖ. πᾶσιν οὖν μετανοοῦσιν ἀφίει ὁ κύριος, ἐὰν μετανοήσωσιν εἰς ἑνότητα θεοῦ καὶ συνέδριον τοῦ ἐπισκόπου. πιστεύω τῇ χάριτι Ἰησοῦ Χριστοῦ, ὃς λύσει ἀφ' ὑμῶν πάντα δεσμόν. 2. παρακαλῶ δὲ ὑμᾶς μηδὲν κατ' ἐριθείαν πράσσειν, ἀλλὰ κατὰ χριστομαθίαν. ἐπεὶ ἤκουσά τινων λεγόντων, ὅτι ἐὰν μὴ ἐν τοῖς ἀρχείοις εὕρω ἐν τῷ εὐαγγελίῳ οὐ πιστεύω· καὶ λέγοντός μου αὐτοῖς ὅτι γέγραπται, ἀπεκρίθησάν μοι ὅτι πρόκειται. ἐμοὶ δὲ ἀρχεῖά ἐστιν Ἰησοῦς Χριστός, τὰ ἄθικτα ἀρχεῖα ὁ σταυρὸς αὐτοῦ καὶ ὁ θάνατος καὶ ἡ ἀνάστασις αὐτοῦ καὶ ἡ πίστις ἡ δι' αὐτοῦ, ἐν οἷς θέλω ἐν τῇ προσευχῇ ὑμῶν δικαιωθῆναι.

## IX

1. Καλοὶ καὶ οἱ ἱερεῖς, κρεῖσσον δὲ ὁ ἀρχιερεὺς ὁ πεπιστευμένος τὰ ἅγια τῶν ἁγίων, ὃς μόνος πεπίστευται τὰ κρυπτὰ τοῦ θεοῦ· αὐτὸς ὢν θύρα τοῦ πατρός, δι' ἧς εἰσέρχονται Ἀβραὰμ καὶ Ἰσαὰκ καὶ Ἰακὼβ καὶ οἱ προφῆται καὶ ἀπόστολοι καὶ ἡ ἐκκλησία. ΄πάντα ταῦτα εἰς ἑνότητα θεοῦ. 2. ἐξαίρετον δέ τι ἔχει τὸ εὐαγγέλιον, τὴν παρουσίαν τοῦ σωτῆρος, κυρίου ἡμῶν Ἰησοῦ Χριστοῦ, τὸ πάθος αὐτοῦ, καὶ τὴν ἀνάσασιν. οἱ γὰρ ἀγαπητοὶ προφῆται κατήγγειλαν εἰς αὐτόν· τὸ δὲ εὐαγγέλιον ἀπάρτισμά ἐστιν ἀφθαρσίας. ΄πάντα ὁνοῦ καλά ἐστιν, ἐὰν ἐν ἀγάπῃ πιστεύητε.

## X

1. Ἐπειδὴ κατὰ τὴν προσευχὴν ὑμῶν καὶ κατὰ τὰ σπλάγνα, ἃ ἔχετε ἐν Χριστῷ Ἰησοῦ, ἀπηγγέλη μοι εἰρηνεύειν τὴν ἐκκλησίαν τὴν ἐν Ἀντιοχείᾳ τῆς Συρίας, πρέπον ἐστὶν ὑμῖν ὡς ἐκκλησίᾳ θεοῦ, χειροτονῆσαι διάκονον εἰς τὸ πρεσβεῦσαι ἐκεῖ θεοῦ πρεσβείαν, εἰς τὸ συγχαρῆναι αὐτοῖς ἐπὶ τὸ αὐτὸ γενομένοις καὶ δοξάσαι τὸ ὄνομα. 2. μακάριος ἐν Ἰησοῦ Χριστῷ, ὃς καταξιωθήσεται τῆς τοιαύτης διακονίας, καὶ ὑμεῖς δοξασθήσεσθε. θέλουσιν δὲ ὑμῖν οὐκ ἔστιν ἀδύνατον ὑπὲρ ὀνόματος θεοῦ, ὡς καὶ αἱ ἔγγιστα ἐκκλησίαι ἔπεμψαν ἐπισκόπους, αἱ δὲ πρεσβυτέρους καὶ διακόνους.

## XI

1. Περὶ δὲ Φίλωνος τοῦ διακόνου ἀπο Κιλικίας, ἀνδρὸς μεμαρτυρημένου, ὃς καὶ νῦν ἐν λόγῳ θεοῦ ὑπηρετεῖ μοι ἅμα Ῥέῳ Ἀγθόποδι, ἀνδρὶ ἐκλεκτῷ, ὃς ἀπὸ Συρίας μοι ἀκολουθεῖ ἀποταξάμενος τῷ βίῳ, οἳ καὶ μαρτυροῦσιν ὑμῖν, κἀγὼ τῷ θεῷ εὐχαριστῶ ὑπὲρ ὑμῶν, ὅτι ἐδέξασθε αὐτούς, ὡς καὶ ὑμᾶς ὁ κύριος· οἱ δὲ ἀτιμάσαντες αὐτοὺς λυτρωθείησαν ἐν τῇ χάριτι τοῦ Ἰησοῦ Χριστοῦ. 2. ἀσπάζεται ὑμᾶς ἡ ἀγάπη τῶν ἀδελφῶν τῶν ἐν Τρωάδι· ὅθεν καὶ γράφω ὑμῖν διὰ Βούρρου πεμφθέντός ἅμα ἐμοὶ ἀπὸ Ἐφεσίων καὶ Σμυρναίων εἰς λόγον τιμῆς. τιμήσει αὐτοὺς ὁ κύριος Ἰησοῦς Χριστός, εἰς ὃν ἐλπίζουσιν σαρκί, ψυχῇ, πνεύματι, πίσει, ἀγάπῃ, ὁμονοίᾳ. ἔρρωσθε ἐν Χριστῷ Ἰησοῦ, τῇ κοινῇ ἐλπίδι ἡμῶν.

# The Epistle of Ignatius to the Smyrnaeans

## Chapter. Prologue

Ignatius, who is also Theophorus, to the church of God the Father and of Jesus Christ the Beloved, which hath been mercifully endowed with every grace, being filled with faith and love and lacking in no grace, most reverend and bearing holy treasures; to the church which is in Smyrna of Asia, in a blameless spirit and in the word of God abundant greeting.

## Chapter. 1

I give glory to Jesus Christ the God who bestowed such wisdom upon you; for I have perceived that ye are established in faith immovable, being as it were nailed on the cross of the Lord Jesus Christ, in flesh and in spirit, and firmly grounded in love in the blood of Christ, fully persuaded as touching our Lord that He is truly of the race of David according to the flesh, but Son of God by the Divine will and power, truly born of a virgin and baptized by John that all righteousness might be fulfilled by Him,

truly nailed up in the flesh for our sakes under Pontius Pilate and Herod the tetrarch (of which fruit are we--that is, of His most blessed passion); that He might set up an ensign unto all the ages through His resurrection, for His saints and faithful people, whether among Jews or among Gentiles, in one body of His Church.

## Chapter. 2

For He suffered all these things for our sakes [that we might be salved]; and He suffered truly, as also He raised Himself truly; not as certain unbelievers say, that He suffered in semblance, being themselves mere semblance. And according as their opinions are, so shall it happen to them, for they are without body and demon-like.

## Chapter. 3

For I know and believe that He was in the flesh even after the resurrection;

and when He came to Peter and his company, He said to them, Lay hold and handle me, and see that I am not a demon without a body. And straightway they touched Him, and they believed, being joined unto His flesh and His blood. Wherefore also they despised death, nay they were found superior to death. And after His resurrection He [both ate with them and drank with them as one in the flesh, though spiritually He was united with the Father.

## Chapter. 4

But these things I warn you, dearly beloved, knowing that ye yourselves are so minded. Howbeit I watch over you betimes to protect you from wild beasts in human form--men whom not only should ye not receive, but, if it were possible, not so much as meet [them]; only pray ye for them, if haply they may repent. This indeed is difficult, but Jesus Christ, our true life, hath power over it.

For if these things were done by our Lord in semblance, then am I also a prisoner in semblance. And why then have I delivered myself over to death, unto fire, unto sword, unto wild beasts? But near to the sword, near to God; in company with wild beasts, in company with God. Only let it be in the name of Jesus Christ, so that we may suffer together with Him. I endure all things, seeing that He Himself enableth me, who is perfect Man.

## Chapter. 5

But certain persons ignorantly deny Him, or rather have been denied by Him, being advocates of death rather than of the truth; and they have not been persuaded by the prophecies nor by the law of Moses, nay nor even to this very hour by the Gospel, nor by the sufferings of each of us severally; for they are of the same mind also concerning us.

For what profit is it [to me], if a man praiseth me, but blasphemeth my Lord, not confessing that He was a bearer of flesh? Yet he that affirmeth not this, doth thereby deny Him altogether, being himself a bearer of a corpse.

But their names, being unbelievers, I have not thought fit to record in writing--nay, far be it from me even to remember them, until they repent and return to the passion, which is our resurrection.

## Chapter. 6

Let no man be deceived. Even the heavenly beings and the glory of the angels and the rulers visible and invisible, if they believe not in the blood of Christ [who is God], judgment awaiteth them also. He that receiveth let him receive. Let not office puff up any man; for faith and love are all in all, and nothing is preferred before them.

But mark ye those who hold strange doctrine touching the grace of Jesus Christ which came to us, how that they are contrary to the mind of God. They have no care for love, none for the widow, none for the orphan, none for the afflicted, none for the prisoner, none for the hungry or thirsty. They abstain from eucharist (thanksgiving) and prayer, because they allow not that the eucharist is the flesh of our Savior Jesus Christ, which flesh suffered for our sins, and which the Father of His goodness raised up.

## Chapter. 7

They therefore that gainsay the good gift of God perish by their questionings. But it were expedient for them to have love, that they may also rise again.

It is therefore meet that ye should abstain from such, and not speak of them either privately or in public; but should give heed to the Prophets, and especially to the Gospel, wherein the passion is shown unto us and the resurrection is accomplished.

## Chapter. 8

[But] shun divisions, as the beginning of evils. Do ye all follow your bishop, as Jesus Christ followed the Father, and the presbytery as the Apostles; and to the deacons pay respect, as to God's commandment. Let no man do aught of things pertaining to the Church apart from the bishop. Let that be held a valid eucharist which is under the bishop or one to whom he shall have committed it.

Wheresoever the bishop shall appear, there let the people be; even as where Jesus may be, there is the universal Church. It is not lawful apart from the bishop either to baptize or to hold a love-feast; but whatsoever he shall approve, this is well-pleasing also to God; that everything which ye do may be sure and valid.

## Chapter. 9

It is reasonable henceforth that we wake to soberness, while we have [still] time to repent and turn to God. It is good to recognize God and the bishop. He that honoreth the bishop is honored of God; he that doeth aught without the knowledge of the bishop rendereth service to the devil.

May all things therefore abound unto you in grace, for ye are worthy. Ye refreshed me in all things, and Jesus Christ shall refresh you. In my absence and in my presence ye cherished me. May God recompense you; for whose sake if ye endure all things, ye shall attain unto Him.

## Chapter. 10

Philo and Rhaius Agathopus, who followed me in the cause of God, ye did well to receive as ministers of [Christ] God; who also give thanks to the Lord for you, because ye refreshed them in every way. Nothing shall be lost to you.

My spirit is devoted for you, as also are my bonds, which ye despised not, neither were ashamed of them. Nor shall He, who is perfect faithfulness, be ashamed of you, even Jesus Christ.

## Chapter. 11

Your prayer sped forth unto the church which is in Antioch of Syria; whence coming a prisoner in most godly bonds I salute all men, though I am not worthy to belong to it, being the very last of them. By the Divine will was this vouchsafed to me, not of my own complicity, but by God's grace, which I pray may be given to me perfectly, that through your prayers I may attain unto God.

Therefore that your work may be perfected both on earth and in heaven, it is meet that your church should appoint, for the honor of God, an ambassador of God that he may go as far as Syria and congratulate them because they are at peace, and have recovered their proper stature, and their proper bulk hath been restored to them.

It seemed to me therefore a fitting thing that ye should send one of your own people with a letter, that he might join with them in giving glory for the calm which by God's will had overtaken them, and because they were already reaching a haven through your prayers. Seeing ye are perfect, let your counsels also be perfect; for if ye desire to do well, God is ready to grant the means.

## Chapter. 12

The love of the brethren which are in Troas saluteth you; from whence also I write to you by the hand of Burrhus, whom ye sent with me jointly with the Ephesians your brethren. He hath refreshed me in all ways. And I would that all imitated him, for he is an ensample of the ministry of God. The Divine grace shall requite him in all things.

I salute your godly bishop and your venerable presbytery [and] my fellow-servants the deacons, and all of you severally and in a body, in the name of Jesus Christ, and in His flesh and blood, in His passion and resurrection, which was both carnal and spiritual, in the unity of God and of yourselves. Grace to you, mercy, peace, patience, always.

## Chapter. 13

I salute the households of my brethren with their wives and children, and the virgins who are called widows. I bid you farewell in the power of the Father. Philo, who is with me, saluteth you.

I salute the household of Tavia, and I pray that she may be grounded in faith and love both of flesh and of spirit. I salute Alce, a name very dear to me, and Daphnus the incomparable, and Eutecnus, and all by name. Fare ye well in the grace of God.

# GREEK

# ΣΜΥΡΝΑΙΟΙΣ ΙΓΝΑΤΙΟΣ

Ἰγνάτιος, ὁ καὶ Θεοφόρος, ἐκκλησίᾳ θεοῦ πατρὸς καὶ τοῦ ἠγαπημένου Ἰησοῦ Χριστοῦ, ἠλεημένῃ ἐν παντὶ χαρίσματι, πεπληρωμένῃ ἐν πίστει καὶ ἀγάπῃ, ἀνυστερήτῳ οὔσῃ παντὸς χαρίσματος, θεοπρεπεστάτῃ καὶ ἁγιοφόρῳ, τῇ οὔσῃ ἐν Σμύρνῃ τῆς Ἀσίας, ἐν ἀμώμῳ πνεύματι καὶ λόγῳ θεοῦ πλεῖστα χαίρειν.

## I

1. Δοξάζω Ἰησοῦν Χριστὸν θεὸν τὸν οὕτως ὑμᾶς σοφίσαντα· ἐνόησα γὰρ ὑμᾶς κατηρτισμένους ἐν ἀκινήτῳ πίστει, ὥσπερ καθηλωμένους ἐν τῷ σταυρῷ τοῦ κυρίου Ἰησοῦ Χριστοῦ σαρκί τε καὶ πνεύματι καὶ ἡδρασμένους ἐν ἀγάπῃ ἐν τῷ αἵματι Χριστοῦ, πεπληροφορημένους εἰς τὸν κύριον ἡμῶν, ἀληθῶς ὄντα ἐκ γένους Δαυεὶδ κατὰ σάρκα, υἱὸν θεοῦ κατὰ θέλημα καὶ δύναμιν θεοῦ, γεγεννημένον ἀληθῶς ἐκ παρθένου, βεβαπτισμένον ὑπὸ Ἰωάννου, ἵνα πληρωθῇ πᾶσα δικαιοσύνη ὑπ' αὐτοῦ· 2. ἀληθῶς ἐπὶ Ποντίου Πιλάτου καὶ Ἡρώδου τετράρχου καθηλωμένον ὑπέρ ἡμῶν ἐν σαρκί, ἀφ' οὗ καρποῦ ἡμεῖς ἀπό τοῦ θεομακαρίστου αὐτοῦ πάθους, ἵνα ἄρῃ σύσσημον εἰς τοὺς αἰῶνας διὰ τῆς ἀναστάσεως εἰς τοὺς ἁγίους καὶ πιστοὺς αὐτοῦ, εἴτε ἐν Ἰουδαίοις εἴτε ἐν ἔθνεσιν, ἐν ἑνὶ σώματι τῆς ἐκκλησίας αὐτοῦ.

## II

1. Ταῦτα γὰρ πάντα ἔπαθεν δι' ἡμᾶς, ἵνα σωθῶμεν· καὶ ἀληθῶς ἔπαθεν, ὡς καὶ ἀληθῶς ἀνέστησεν ἑαυτόν, οὐχ ὥσπερ ἄπιστοί

τινες λέγουσιν, τὸ δοκεῖν αὐτὸν πεπονθέναι, αὐτοὶ τὸ δοκεῖν ὄντες· καὶ καθὼς φρονοῦσιν, καὶ συμβήσεται αὐτοῖς, οὖσιν ἀσωμάτοις καὶ δαιμονικοῖς.

## III

1. Ἐγὼ γὰρ καὶ μετὰ τὴν ἀνάστασιν ἐν σαρκὶ αὐτὸν οἶδα καὶ πιστεύω ὄντα. 2. καὶ ὅτε πρὸς τοὺς περὶ Πέτρον ἦλθεν, ἔφη αὐτοῖς· Λάβετε, ψηλαφήσατέ με καὶ ἴδετε, ὅτι οὐκ εἰμὶ δαιμόνιον ἀσώματον. καὶ εὐθὺς αὐτοῦ ἥψαντο καὶ ἐπίστευσαν, καρθέντες τῇ σαρκὶ αὐτοῦ καὶ τῷ πνεύματι. διὰ τοῦτο καὶ θανάτου κατεφρόνησαν, ηὑρέθησαν δὲ ὑπὲρ θάνατον. 3. μετὰ δὲ τὴν ἀνάσασιν συνέφαγεν αὐτοῖς καὶ συνέπιεν ὡς σαρκικός, καίπερ πνευματικῶς ἡνωμένος τῷ πατρί.

## IV

1. Ταῦτα δὲ παραινῶ ὑμῖν, ἀγαπητοί, εἰδὼς ὅτι καὶ ὑμεῖς οὕτως ἔχετε. προφυλάσσω δὲ ὑμᾶς ἀπὸ τῶν θηρίων τῶν ἀνθρωπομόρφων, οὓς οὐ μόνον δεῖ ὑμᾶς μὴ παραδέχεσθαι, ἀλλ᾽ εἰ δυνατὸν μηδὲ συναντᾶν, μόνον δὲ προεύχεσθε ὑπὲρ αὐτῶν, ἐάν πως μεταμοήσωσιν, ὅπερ δύσκολον, τούτου δὲ ἔχει ἐξουσίαν Ἰησοῦς Χριστός, τὸ ἀληθινὸν ἡμῶν ζῆν. 2. εἰ γὰρ τὸ δοκεῖν ταῦτα ἐπράχθη ὑπὸ του κυρίου ἡμῶν, κἀγὼ τὸ δοκεῖν δέδεμαι. τί δὲ καὶ ἑαυτὸν ἔκδοτον δέδωκα τῷ θανάτῳ, πρὸς πῦρ, πρὸς μάχαιραν, πρὸς θηρία; ἀλλ᾽ ἐγγυς μαχαίρας ἐγγὺς θεοῦ· μόνον ἐν τῷ ὀνόματι Ἰησοῦ Χριστοῦ εἰς τὸ συμπαθεῖν αὐτῷ πάντα ὑπομένω, αὐτοῦ με ἐνδυναμοῦντος τοῦ τελείου ἀνθρώπου.

## V

1. Ὅν τινες ἀγνοοῦντες ἀρνοῦνται, μᾶλλον δὲ ἠρνήθησαν ὑπ' αὐτοῦ, ὄντες συνήγοροι του θανάτου μᾶλλον ἢ τῆς ἀληθείας· οὓς οὐκ ἔπεισαν αἱ προφητεῖαι οὐδὲ ὁ νόμος Μωύσεως, ἀλλ' οὐδὲ μέχρι νῦν τὸ εὐαγγέλιον, οὐδὲ τὰ ἡμέτερα τῶν κατ' ἄνδρα παθήματα. 2. καὶ γὰρ περὶ ἡμῶν τὸ αὐτὸ φρονοῦσιν. τί γάρ με ὠφελεῖ τις, εἰ ἐμὲ ἐπαινεῖ, τὸν δὲ κύριόν μου βλασφημεῖ, μὴ ὁμολογῶν αὐτὸν σαρκοφόρον; ὁ δὲ τοῦτο λέγων τελείως αὐτὸν ἀπήρνηται, ὢν νεκροφόρος. 3. τὰ δὲ ὀνόματα αὐτῶν, ὄντα ἄπιστα, οὐκ ἔδοξέν μοι ἐγγράψαι. οὗ μετανοήσωσιν εἰς τὸ πάθος, ὅ ἐστιν ἡμῶν ἀνάστασις.

## VI

1. Μηδεὶς πλανάσθω· καὶ τὰ ἐπουράνια καὶ ἡ δόξα τῶν ἀγγέλων καὶ οἱ ἄρχοντες ὁρατοί τε καὶ ἀόρατοι, ἐὰν μὴ πιστεύσωσιν εἰς τὸ αἷμα Χριστοῦ, μηδένα φυσιούτω· καταμάθετε δὲ τοὺς ἑτεροδοξοῦντας εἰς τὴν χάριν Ἰησοῦ Χριστοῦ τὴν εἰς ἡμᾶς ἐλθοῦσαν, πῶς ἐναντίοι εἰσὶν τῇ γνώμῃ τοῦ θεοῦ. περὶ ἀγάπης οὐ μέλει αὐτοῖς, οὐ περὶ χήρας, οὐ περὶ ὀρφανοῦ, οὐ περὶ θλιβομένου, οὐ περὶ δεδεμένου ἢ λελυμένου, οὐ περὶ πεινῶντος ἢ διψῶντος.

## VII

1. Εὐχαριστίας καὶ προσευχῆς ἀπέχονται, διὰ τὸ μὴ ὁμολογεῖν τὴν εὐχαριστίαν σάρκα εἶναι τοῦ σωτῆρος ἡμῶν Ἰησοῦ Χριστοῦ τὴν ὑπὲρ τῶν ἁμαρτιῶν ἡμῶν παθοῦσαν, ἣν τῇ χρηστότητι ὁ θεοῦ συζητοῦντες ἀποθνήσουσιν· συνέφερεν δὲ αὐτοῖς ἀγαπᾶν, ἵνα καὶ ἀναστῶσιν. 2. πρέπον ἐστὶν ἀπέχθαι τῶν τοιούτων καὶ

μήτε κατ' ἰδίαν περὶ αὐτῶν λαλεῖν μήτε κοινῇ, προσέχειν δὲ τοῖς προφήταις, ἐξαιρέτως δὲ τῷ εὐαγγελίῳ, ἐν ᾧ τὸ πάθος ἡμῖν δεδήλωται καὶ ἡ ἀνάστασις τετελείωται. τοὺς δὲ μερισμοὺς φεύγετε ὡς ἀρχὴν κακῶν.

## VIII

1. Πάντες τῷ ἐπισκόπῳ ἀκολουθεῖτε, ὡς Ἰησοῦς Χριστὸς τῷ πατρί, καὶ τῷ πρεσβυτερίῳ ὡς τοῖς ἀποστόλοις. τοὺς δὲ διακόνους ἐντρέπεσθε ὡς θεοῦ ἐντολήν. μηδεὶς χωρὶς τοῦ ἐπισκόπου τι πρασσέτω τῶν ἀνηκόντων εἰς τὴν ἐκκλησίαν. ἐκείνη βεβαία εὐχαριστία ἡγείσθω, ἡ ὑπὸ ἐπίσοπον οὖσα ἢ ᾧ ἂν αὐτὸς ἐπιτρέψῃ. 2. ὅπου ἂν φανῇ ὁ ἐπίσκοπος, ἐκεῖ τὸ πλῆθος ἤτω, ὥσπερ ὅπου ἂν ᾖ Ἰησοῦς Χριστός, ἐκεῖ ἡ καθολικὴ ἐκκλησία. οὐκ ἐξόν ἐστιν χωρὶς τοῦ ἐπισκόπου οὔτε βαπτίζειν οὔτε ἀγάπην ποιεῖν· ἀλλ' ὃ ἂν ἐκεῖνος δοκιμάσῃ, τοῦτο καὶ τῷ θεῷ εὐάρεστον, ἵνα ἀσφαλὲς ᾖ καὶ βέβαιον πᾶν ὃ πράσσετε.

## IX

1. Εὔλογόν ἐστιν λοιπὸν ἀνανῆψαι ἡμᾶς, ὡς ἔτι καιρὸν ἔχομεν εἰς θεὸν μεταμοεῖν. καλῶς ἔχει, θεὸν καὶ ἐπίσκοπον εἰδέναι. ὁ τιμῶν ἐπίσκοπον ὑπὸ θεοῦ τετίμηται· ὁ λάθρα ἐπισκόποου τι πράσσων τῷ διαβόλῳ λατρεύει. 2. πάντα οὖν ὑμῖν ἐν χάριτι περισσευέτω· ἄξιοι γάρ ἐστε. κατὰ πάντα με ἀνεπαύσατε, καὶ ὑμᾶς Ἰησοῦς Χριστός. ἀπόντα με καὶ πάροντα ἠγαπήσατε. ἀμοιβὴ ὑμῖν ὁ θεός, δι' ὃν πάντα ὑπομένοντες αὐτοῦ τεύξεσθε.

## X

1. Φίλωνα καὶ Ῥέον Ἀγαθόπουν, οἳ ἐπηκολούθησάν μοι εἰς λόγον θεοῦ, καλῶς ἐποιήσαε ὑποδεξάμενοι ὡς διακόνους θεοῦ· οἳ καὶ εὐχαριστοῦσιν τῷ κυρίῳ ὑπὲρ ὑμῶν, ὅτι αὐτοὺς ἀνεπαύσατε κατὰ πάντα τρόπον. οὐδὲν ὑμῖν οὐ μὴ ἀπολεῖται. 2. ἀντίψυχον ὑμῶν τὸ πνεῦμά μου καὶ τὰ δεσμά μου, ἃ οὐχ ὑπερηφανήσατε οὐδὲ ἐπῃσσύνθητε. οὐδὲ ὑμᾶς ἐαισχυνθήσεται ἡ τελεία ἐλπίς, Ἰησοῦς Χριστός.

## XI

1. Ἡ προσευχὴ ὑμῶν ἀπῆλθεν ἐπι τὴν ἐκκλησίαν τὴν ἐν Ἀντιοχείᾳ τῆς Συρίας, ὅθεν δεδεμένος θεοπρεπεστάτοις δεσμοῖς πάντας ἀσπάζομαι, οὐκ ὢν ἄξιος ἐκεῖθεν εἶναι, ἔσχατος αὐτῶν ὢν· κατὰ θέλημα δὲ κατηξιώθην, οὐκ ἐκ συνειδότος ἀλλ᾽ ἐκ χάριτος θεοῦ· ἣν εὔχομαι τελείαν μοι δοθῃναι, ἵνα ἐν τῇ πορσευχῇ ὑμῶν θεοῦ ἐπιτύχω. 2. ἵνα οὖν ὑμῶν τέλειον γένηται τὸ ἔργον καὶ ἐπὶ γῆς καὶ ἐν οὐρανῷ, πρέπει εἰς τιμὴν θεοῦ χειροτονῆσαι τὴν ἐκκλησίαν ὑμῶν θεοπρεσβεύτην, εἰς τὸ γενόμενον ἐν Συρίᾳ συγχαρῆναι αὐτοῖς, ὅτι εἰρηνεύουσιν καὶ ἀπέλαβον τὸ ἴδιον μέγεθος καὶ ἀπεκατεστάθη αὐτοῖς τὸ ἴδιον σωματεῖον. 3. ἐφάνη μοι οὖν θεοῦ ἄξιον πρᾶγμα, πέμψαι τινὰ τῶν ὑμετέρων μετ᾽ ἐπειστολῆς, ἵνα συνδοξάσῃ τὴν κατὰ θεὸν αὐτοῖς γενομένην εὐδίαν, καὶ ὅτι λιμένος ἤδη ἐτύγχανον τῇ προσευχῇ ὑμῶν. τέλειοι ὄντες τέλεια καὶ φρονεῖτε. θέλουσιν γὰρ ὑμῖν εὖ πράσσειν θεὸς ἕτοιμος εἰς τὸ παρέχειν.

## XII

1. Ἀσπάζεται ὑμᾶς ἡ ἀγάπη τῶν ἀδελφῶν τῶν ἐν Τρωάδι ὅθεν καὶ γράφω ὑμῖν διὰ Βούρρου, ὃν ἀπεστείλατε μετ' ἐμοῦ ἅμα Ἐφεσίοις, τοῖς ἀδελφοῖς ὑμῶν, ὃς κατὰ πάντα με ἀνέπαυσεν. καὶ ὄφελον πάντες αὐτὸν ἐμιμοῦντο, ὄντα ἐξεμπλάριον θεοῦ διακονίας. ἀμείψεται αὐτὸν ἡ χάρις κατὰ πάντα. 2. ἀσπάζομαι τὸν ἀξιόθεον ἐπίσκοπον καὶ θεοπρεπὲς πρεσβυτέριον καὶ τοὺς συνδούλους μου διακόνους καὶ τοὺς κατ' ἄνδρα καὶ κοινῇ πάντας ἐν ὀνόματι Ἰησοῦ Χριστοῦ καὶ τῇ σαρκὶ αὐτοῦ καὶ τῷ αἵματι, πάθει τε καὶ ἀναστάσει σαρκικῇ τε καὶ πνευματικῇ, ἐν ἑνότητι θεοῦ καὶ ὑμῶν. χάρις ὑμῖν, ἔλεος, ἐρήνη, ὑπομοὴ διὰ παντός.

## XIII

1. Ἀσπάζομαι τοὺς οἴκους τῶν ἀδελφῶν μου σὺν γυναιξὶ καὶ τένοις καὶ τὰς παρθένους τὰς λεγομένας χήρας. ἔρωσθέ μοι ἐν δυνάμει πατρός. ἀσπάζεται ὑμᾶς Φίλων σὺν ἐμοὶ ὤν. 2. ἀσπάζομαι τὸν οἶκον Ταουΐας, ἣν εὔχομαι ἑδρᾶσθαι πίστει καὶ ἀγάπῃ σαρκικῇ τε καὶ πνευματικῇ. ἀσπάζομαι Ἄλκην, τὸ ποθητόν μοι ὄνομα, καὶ Δάφνον τὸν ἀσύγκριτον καὶ Εὔτεκνον καὶ πάντας κατ' ὄνομα. ἔρρωσθε ἐν χάριτι θεοῦ.

# The Epistle of Ignatius to Polycarp

## Chapter. Prologue

Ignatius, who is also Theophorus, unto Polycarp who is bishop of the church of the Smyrnaens or rather who hath for his bishop God the Father and Jesus Christ, abundant greeting.

## Chapter. 1

Welcoming thy godly mind which is grounded as it were on an immovable rock, I give exceeding glory that it hath been vouchsafed me to see thy blameless face,

whereof I would fain have joy in God. I exhort thee in the grace wherewith thou art clothed to press forward in thy course and to exhort all men that they may be saved. Vindicate thine office in all diligence of flesh and of spirit. Have a care for union, than which there is nothing better. Bear all men, as the Lord also beareth thee. Suffer all men in love, as also thou doest.

Give thyself to unceasing prayers. Ask for larger wisdom than thou hast. Be watchful, and keep thy spirit from slumbering. Speak to each man severally after the manner of God. Bear the maladies of all, as a perfect athlete. where there is more toil, there is much gain.

## Chapter. 2

If thou lovest good scholars, this is not thankworthy in thee. Rather bring the more pestilent to submission by gentleness. All wounds are not healed by the same salve. Allay sharp pains by fomentations.

Be thou prudent as the serpent in all things and guileless always as the dove. Therefore art thou made of flesh and spirit, that thou mayest humor the things which appear before thine eyes; and as for the invisible things, pray thou that they may be revealed unto thee; that thou mayest be lacking in nothing, but mayest abound in every spiritual gift.

The season requireth thee, as pilots require winds or as a storm-tossed mariner a haven, that it may attain unto God. Be sober, as God's athlete. The prize is incorruption and life eternal, concerning which thou also art persuaded. In all things I am devoted to thee--I and my bonds which thou didst cherish.

## Chapter. 3

Let not those that seem to be plausible and yet teach strange doctrine dismay thee. Stand thou firm, as an anvil when it is smitten. It is the part of a great athlete to receive blows and be victorious. But especially must we for God's sake endure all things, that He also may endure us.

Be thou more diligent than thou art. Mark the seasons. Await Him that is above every season, the Eternal, the Invisible, who became visible for our sake, the Impalpable, the Impassible, who suffered for our sake, who endured in all ways for our sake.

## Chapter. 4

Let not widows be neglected. After the Lord be thou their protector. Let nothing be done without thy consent; neither do thou anything without the consent of God, as indeed thou doest not. Be steadfast.

Let meetings be held more frequently. Seek out all men by name.

Despise not slaves, whether men or women. Yet let not these again be puffed up, but let them serve the more faithfully to the glory of God, that they may obtain a better freedom from God. Let them not desire to be set free at the public cost, lest they be found slaves of lust.

## Chapter. 5

Flee evil arts, or rather hold thou discourse about these. Tell my sisters to love the Lord and to be content with their husbands in flesh and in spirit. In like manner also charge my brothers in the name of Jesus Christ to love their wives, as the Lord loved the Church.

If any one is able to abide in chastity to the honor of the flesh of the Lord, let him so abide without boasting. If he boast, he is lost; and if it be known beyond the bishop, he is polluted. It becometh men and women too, when they marry, to unite themselves with the consent of the bishop, that the marriage may be after the Lord and not after concupiscence. Let all things be done to the honor of God.

## Chapter. 6

Give ye heed to the bishop, that God also may give heed to you. I am devoted to those who are subject to the bishop, the presbyters, the deacons. May it be granted me to have my portion with them in the presence of God. Toil together one with another, struggle together, run together, suffer together, lie down together, rise up together, as God's stewards and assessors and ministers.

Please the Captain in whose army ye serve, from whom also ye will receive your pay. Let none of you be found a deserter. Let your baptism abide with you as your shield; your faith as your helmet; your love as your spear; your patience as your body armor. Let your works be your deposits, that ye may receive your assets due to you. Be ye therefore long-suffering one with another in gentleness, as God is with you. May I have joy of you always.

## Chapter. 7

Seeing that the church which is in Antioch of Syria hath peace, as it hath been reported to me, through your prayers, I myself also have been the more comforted since God hath banished my care; if so be I may through suffering attain unto God, that I may be found a disciple through your intercession.

It becometh thee, most blessed Polycarp, to call together a godly council and to elect some one among you who is very dear to you and zealous also, who shall be fit to bear the name of God's courier--to appoint him, I say, that he may go to Syria and glorify your zealous love unto the glory of God.

A Christian hath no authority over himself, but giveth his time to God. This is God's work, and yours also, when ye shall complete it: for I trust in the Divine grace, that ye are ready for an act of well doing which is meet for God. Knowing the fervor of your sincerity, I have exhorted you in a short letter.

## Chapter. 8

Since I have not been able to write to all the churches, by reason of my sailing suddenly from Troas to Neapolis, as the Divine will enjoineth, thou shalt write to the churches in front, as one possessing the mind of God, to the intent that they also may do this same thing--let those who are able send messengers, and the rest letters by the persons who are sent by thee, that ye may be glorified by an ever memorable deed--for this is worthy of thee.

I salute all by name, and especially the wife of Epitropus with her whole household and her children's. I salute Attalus my beloved. I salute him that shall be appointed to go to Syria. Grace shall be with him always, and with Polycarp who sendeth him.

I bid you farewell always in our God Jesus Christ, in whom abide ye in the unity and supervision of God. I salute Alce, a name very dear to me. Fare ye well in the Lord.

# GREEK

# ΠΡΟΣ ΠΟΛΥΚΑΡΠΟΝ ΙΓΝΑΤΙΟΣ

Ἰγνάτιος, ὁ καὶ Θεοφόρος, Πουκάρπῳ ἐπισκόπῳ ἐκκλησίας Σμυρναίων, μᾶλλον ἐπισκοπημένῳ ὑπὸ θεοῦ πατρὸς καὶ κυρίου Ἰησοῦ Χριστοῦ, πλεῖστα χαίρειν.

## I

1. Ἀποδεχόμενός σου τὴν ἐν θεῷ γνώμην ἡδρασμένην ὡς ἐπὶ πέτραν ἀκίνητον, ὑπερδοξάζω, καταξιωθεὶς τοῦ προσώπου σου τοῦ ἀμώμου, οὗ ὀναίμην ἐν θεῷ. 2. παρακαλῶ σε ἐν χάριτι ᾗ ἐνδέδυσαι, προσθεῖναι τῷ δρόμῳ σου καὶ πάντας παρακαλεῖν, ἵνα σώζωνται. ἐκίκει σου τὸν τόπον ἐν πάσῃ ἐπιμελείᾳ σαρκικῇ τε καὶ πνευματικῇ· τῆς ἑνώσεως φρόντιζε, ἧς οὐδὲν ἄμεινον. πάντας βάσταζε, ὡς καὶ σὲ ὁ κύριος· πάντων ἀνέχου ἐν ἀγάπῃ, ὥσπερ καὶ ποιεῖς. 3. προσευχαῖς σχόλαζε ἀδιαλείπτοις· αἰτοῦ σύνεσιν πλείονα ἧς ἔχεις· γρηγόρει ἀκοίμητον πνεῦμα κεκτημένος. τοῖς κατ' ἄνδρα κατὰ ὁμοήθειαν θεοῦ λάλει· ΄πάντων τὰς νόσους βάσταζε ὡς τέλειος ἀθλητής. ὅπου πλείων κόπος, πολὺ κέρδος.

## II

1. Καλοὺς μαθητὰς ἐὰν φιλῇς, χάρις σοι οὐκ ἔστιν· μᾶλλον τοὺς λοιμοτέρους ἐν πραότητι ὑπότασσε. οὐ πᾶν τραῦμα τῇ αὐτῇ ἐμπλάστρῳ θεραπεύεται. τοὺς παροξυσμοὺς ἐμβροχαῖς παῦε. 2. φρόνιμος γίνου ὡς ὁ ὄφις ἐν ἅπασιν καὶ ἀκέραιος εἰς ἀεὶ ὡς ἡ περιστερά. διὰ τοῦτο σαρκικὸς εἶ καὶ πνευματικός, ἵνα τὰ φαινόμενά σου εἰς πρόσωπον κολακεύῃς· τὰ δὲ ἀόρατα αἴτει

ἵνα σοι φανερωθῇ, ὅπως μηδενὸς λείπῃ καί παντὸς χαρίσματος περισσεύῃς. 3. ὁ καιρὸς ἀπαιτεῖ σε, ὡς κυβερνῆται ἀνένους καὶ ὡς χειμαζόμενος λιμένα, εἰς τὸ θεοῦ ἐπιτυχεῖν. νῆφε, ὡς θεοῦ ἀθλητής· τὸ θέμα ἀφθαρσία καὶ ζωὴ αἰώνιος, περὶ ἧς καὶ σὺ πέπεισαι. κατὰ πάντα σου ἀντιψυχον ἐγὼ καὶ τὰ δεσμά μου, ἃ ἠγάπησας.

## III

1. Οἱ δοκοῦντες ἀξιόπιστοι εἶναι καὶ ἑτεροδιδασκαοῦντες μή σε καταπλησσέτωσαν. στῆθι ἑδραῖος ὡς ἄκμων τυπτόμενος. μεγάλου ἐστιν ἀθλητοῦ τὸ δέρεσθαι καὶ νικᾶν. μάλιστα δὲ ἕνεκεν θεοῦ πάντα ὑπομένειν ἡμᾶς δεῖ, ἵνα καὶ αὐτὸς ἡμᾶς ὑπομένῃ. 2. πλέον σπουδαῖος γίνου οὗ εἶ. τοὺς καιροὺς καταμάνθανε. τὸν ὑπὲρ καιρὸν προσδόκα, τὸν ἄχρονον, τὸν ἀόρατον, τὸν δι' ἡμᾶς ὁρατόν, τὸν ἀψηλάφητον, τὸν ἀπαθῆ, τὸν δι' ἡμᾶς παθητόν, τὸν κατὰ πάντα τρόπον δι' ἡμᾶς ὑπομείναντα.

## IV

1. Χῆραι μὴ ἀμελείσθωσαν· μετὰ τὸν κύριον σὺ αὐτῶν φροντιστὴς ἔσο. μηδὲν ἄνευ γνώμης σου γινέσθω μηδὲ σὺ ἄνευ θεοῦ τι πρᾶσσε, ὅπερ οὐδὲ πράσσεις· 2. πυκνότερον συναγωγαὶ γινέσθωσαν· ἐξ ὀνόματος πάντας ζήτει. 3. δούλους καὶ δούλας μὴ ὑπερηφάνει· ἀλλὰ μηδὲ αὐτοὶ φυσιούσθωσαν, ἀλλ' εἰς δόξαν θεοῦ πλέον δουλευέτωσαν, ἵνα κρείττονος ἐλευθερίας ἀπό θεοῦ τύχωσιν. μὴ ἐράτωσαν ἀπὸ τοῦ κοινοῦ ἐλευθεροῦσθαι, ἵνα μὴ δοῦλοι εὑρεθῶσιν ἐπιθυμίας.

## V

1. Τὰς κακοτεχνίας φεῦγε, μᾶλλον δὲ περὶ τούτων ὁμιλίαν ποιοῦ. ταῖς ἀδελφαῖς μου προσλάλει, ἀγαπᾶν τὸν κύριον καὶ τοῖς συμβίοις ἀρκεῖσθαι σαρκὶ καὶ πνεύματι. ὁμοίως καὶ τοῖς ἀδελφοῖς μου παράγγελλε ἐν ὀνόματι Ἰησοῦ Χριστοῦ, ἀγαπᾶν τὰς συμβίους ὡς ὁ κύριος τὴν ἐκκλησίαν. 2. εἴ τις δύναται ἐν ἁγνείᾳ μένειν εἰς τιμὴν τῆς σαρκὸς τοῦ κυρίου, ἐν ἀκαυχησίᾳ μενέτω. ἐὰν καυχήσηται, ἀπώλετο, καὶ ἐὰν γνωσθῇ πλέον τοῦ ἐπισκόπου, ἔφθαρται. πρέπει δὲ τοῖς γαμοῦσι καὶ ταῖς γαμουμέαις μετὰ γνώμης τοῦ ἐπισκόπου τὴν ἕνωσιν ποιεῖσθαι, ἵνα ὁ γάμος ᾖ κατὰ κύριον καὶ μὴ κατ' ἐπιθυμίαν. πάντα εἰς τιμὴν θεοῦ γινέσθω.

## VI

1. Τῷ ἐπισκόπῳ προσέχετε, ἵνα καὶ ὁ θεὸς ὑμῖν. ἀνίψυχον ἐγὼ τῶν ὑποτασσομένων τῷ ἐπισκόπῳ, πρεσβυτέροις, διακόνοις· καὶ μετ' αὐτῶν μοι τὸ μέρος γένοιτο σχεῖν ἐν θεῷ. συγκοπιᾶτε, ἀλλήλοις, συναθλεῖτε, συντρέχετε, συμπάσχετε, συγκοιμᾶσθε, συνεγείρεσθε ὡς θεοῦ οἰκονόμοι καὶ πάρεδροι καὶ ὑπηρέται. 2. ἀρέσκετε ᾧ στρατεύεσθε, ἀφ' οὗ καὶ τὰ ὀψώνια κομίζεσθε· μή τις ὑμῶν δεσέρτωρ εὑρεθῇ. τὸ βάπτισμα ὑμῶν μενέτω ὡς ὅπλα, ἡ πίστις ὡς περικεφαλαία, ἡ ἀγάπη ὡς δόρυ, ἡ ὑπομονὴ ὡς πανοπλία. τὰ δεπόσιτα ὑμῶν τὰ ἔργα ὑμῶν, ἵνα τὰ ἄκκεπτα ὑμῶν ἄξια κομίσησθε. μακροθυμήσατε οὖν μετ' ἀλλήλων ἐν πραότητι, ὡς ὁ θεὸς μεθ' ὑμῶν. ὀναίμην ὑμῶν διὰ παντός.

## VII

1. Ἐπειδὴ ἡ ἐκκλησία ἡ ἐν Ἀντιοχείᾳ τῆς Συρίας εἰρηνεύει, ὡς ἐδηλώθη μοι, διὰ τὴν προσευχὴν ὑμῶν, κἀγὼ εὐθυμότερος

ἐγενόμην ἐν ἀμεριμνίᾳ θεοῦ, ἐάνπερ διὰ τοῦ παθεῖν θεοῦ ἐπιτύχω, εἰς τὸ εὑρεθῆναί με ἐν τῇ ἀναστάσει ὑμῶν μαθητήν. 2. πρέπει, Πολύκαρπε, θεομακαριστότατε, συμβούλιον, ἀγαγεῖν θεοπρεπέστατον καὶ χειροτονῆσαί τινα, ὃν ἀγαπητὸν λίαν ἔχετε καὶ ἄοκνον, ὃς δυνήσεται θεοδρόμος καλεῖσθαι· τοῦτον καταξιῶσαι, ἵνα πορευθεὶς εἰς Συρίαν δοξάσῃ ὑμῶν τὴν ἄοκνον εἰς δόξαν θεοῦ· 3. Χριστιανὸς ἑαυτοῦ ἐξουσίαν οὐκ ἔχει, ἀλλὰ θεῷ σχολάζει. τοῦτο τὸ ἔργον θεοῦ ἐστιν καὶ ὑμῶν, ὅταν αὐτὸ ἀπαρτίσητε. πιστεύω γὰρ τῇ χάριτι, ὅτι ἕτοιμοί ἐστε εἰς εὐποιΐαν θεῷ ἀνήκουσαν. εἰδὼς ὑμῶν τὸ σύντονον τῆς ἀληθείας, δι' ὀλίγων ὑμᾶς γραμμάτων παρεκάλεσα.

## VIII

1. Ἐπεὶ πάσαις ταῖς ἐκκλησίαις οὐκ ἠδυνηθην γράψαι διὰ τὸ ἐξαίφνης πλεῖν με ἀπο Τρωάδος εἰς Νεάπολιν, ὡς το θέλημα προστάσσει, γράψεις ταῖς ἔμπροσθεν ἐκκλησίαις, ὡς θεοῦ γνώμην κεκτημένος, εἰς τὸ καὶ αὐτοὺς τὸ αὐτὸ ποιῆσαι, (οἱ μὲν δυνάμενοι πεχοὺς πέμψαι, οἱ δὲ ἐπιστολὰς διὰ τῶν ὑπὸ σου πεμπομένων, ἵνα δοξασθῆτε αἰωνίῳ ἔργῳ,)* ὡς ἄξιος ὤν. 2. ἀσπάζομαι πάντας ἐξ ὀνόματος καὶ τὴν τοῦ Ἐπιτρόπου σὺν ὅλῳ τῷ οἴκῳ αὐτῆς καὶ τῶν τέκνων. ἀσπάζομαι Ἄταλον τὸν ἀγαπητόν μου. ἀσπάζομαι τὸν μέλλοντα καταξιοῦσθαι τοῦ εἰς Συρίαν πορεύεσθαι, ἔσται ἡ χάρις μετ' αὐτοῦ διὰ παντὸς καὶ τοῦ πέμποντος αὐτον Πολυκάρπου. 3. ἐρρῶσθαι ὑμᾶς διὰ παντὸς ἐν θεῷ ἡμῶν Ἰησοῦ Χριστῷ εὔχομαι, ἐν ᾧ διαμείνητε ἐν ἑνότητι θεοῦ καὶ ἐπισκοπῇ. ἀσπάζομαι Ἄλκην, τὸ ποθητόν μοι ὄνομα. ἔρρωσθε ἐν κυρίῳ.